Nancy Cary

The Powerful Potential of Learning Communities
Improving Education for the Future

Oscar T. Lenning and Larry H. Ebbers

ASHE-ERIC Higher Education Report Volume 26, Number 6

D0920269

Prepared by

ERIC Clearinghouse on Higher Education
The George Washington University
URL: www.eriche.org

In cooperation with

Association for the Study
of Higher Education
URL: http://www.tiger.coe.missouri.edu/~ashe

Published by

WASHINGTON DC

Graduate School of Education and Human Development
The George Washington University
URL: www.gwu.edu

Adrianna J. Kezar, Series Editor

Cite as

Lenning, Oscar T., and Larry H. Ebbers. 1999. *The Powerful Potential of Learning Communities: Improving Education for the Future.* ASHE-ERIC Higher Education Report Volume 26, No. 6. Washington, D.C.: The George Washington University, Graduate School of Education and Human Development.

Library of Congress Catalog Card Number 98-88007
ISSN 0884-0040
ISBN 1-878380-86-9

Managing Editor: Lynne J. Scott
Manuscript Editor: Barbara M. Fishel
Cover Design by Michael David Brown, Inc., The Red Door Gallery, Rockport, ME

The ERIC Clearinghouse on Higher Education invites individuals to submit proposals for writing monographs for the *ASHE-ERIC Higher Education Report* series. Proposals must include:
1. A detailed manuscript proposal of not more than five pages.
2. A chapter-by-chapter outline.
3. A 75-word summary to be used by several review committees for the initial screening and rating of each proposal.
4. A vita and a writing sample.

ERIC Clearinghouse on Higher Education
Graduate School of Education and Human Development
The George Washington University
One Dupont Circle, Suite 630
Washington, DC 20036-1183

> *The mission of the ERIC system is to improve American education by increasing and facilitating the use of educational research and information on practice in the activities of learning, teaching, educational decision making, and research, wherever and whenever these activities take place.*

This publication was prepared partially with funding from the Office of Educational Research and Improvement, U.S. Department of Education, under contract no. ED-99-00-0036. The opinions expressed in this report do not necessarily reflect the positions or policies of OERI or the Department.

EXECUTIVE SUMMARY

Why Do We Need Learning Communities?

Too often the concept of community within higher education is paid only lip service, and its potential goes unrealized. But creative new approaches to learning communities are being developed that can greatly improve learning among college students. Building communities of learners creates an environment that can potentially advance a whole society.

The current interest in learning communities has its roots in earlier works. Boyer's principles (1987) of purposeful community, open community, just community, disciplined community, caring community, and celebrative community are important for understanding community in higher education. The introduction of "learning organizations" (Senge 1990) created a new synergy throughout higher education, and "cross-curricular learning communities" stimulated a number of colleges and universities to create special learning communities for students (Gabelnick et al. 1990). Only when a college or university is a true learning organization can it expect to create faculty learning communities and student learning communities that will result in positive outcomes.

Higher education as a community must intentionally develop learning communities that promote and maximize learning—applicable as much to distance learning as to on-site learning. The essence of higher education in both settings is to emphasize learning and collaboration, thereby stimulating learning for individuals and groups.

What Types of Learning Communities Are Important for Higher Education?

Two dimensions of learning communities are important for higher education. *Primary membership* differentiates characteristics the group members have in common; it includes learning organizations, faculty learning communities, and student learning communities. *Primary form of interaction* differentiates group members' method of interaction, such as in-person physical interaction, virtual interaction, or nondirect interaction through correspondence.

Colleges and universities need to consider four basic categories of student learning communities: curricular learning communities, classroom learning communities, residential learning communities, and student-type learning communities. The categories can be meaningfully combined in various ways. For example, any curricular learning community can include a group of students who are living and studying together in the same residence hall.

How Do Learning Communities Contribute to Learning Environments?

Extensive documentary evidence suggests that effective learning communities have important benefits for students and faculty. Benefits for students include higher academic achievement, better retention rates, greater satisfaction with college life, improved quality of thinking and communicating, a better understanding of self and others, and a greater ability to bridge the gap between the academic and social worlds. Faculty benefits include diminished isolation, a shared purpose and cooperation among faculty colleagues, increased curricular integration, a fresh approach to one's discipline, and increased satisfaction with their students' learning.

How Can Learning in Virtual Communities Be Maximized?

With faculty and students linked to the Internet, the stage is set for the formation of a multitude of virtual learning communities, and their use to improve student learning is expanding rapidly. Two principles of good practice for developing such learning communities are to make sure they are student centered and focused on a common goal, and to design the communities to include preparation, planning, and reflection (Treuer and Belote 1997). Other principles of good practice for electronic communities pertain to curriculum and instruction, institutional context and commitment to role and mission, faculty support, resources for learning, students and student services, and commitment to support, evaluation, and assessment (Johnstone and Krauth 1996). Appropriate assessment is an important factor, but research and development in this area is still in its infancy (Powers and Mitchell 1997).

What Important Questions Should Be Considered in Developing and Implementing College Student Learning Communities?

Evidence suggests that most learning communities can be modified to have even greater positive effects on students and their learning. It also suggests that for learning communities to be attractive to faculty, effective and appropriate incentives for faculty participation must be provided. The following questions and answers address anticipated problems in establishing student learning communities:

- *What if faculty are not interested in campus-based learning communities?* Assemble a small group of faculty and student affairs staff to determine feasibility for the campus; enlist the support of top administrators.
- *What if lectures are the predominant teaching method and active learning is not emphasized?* Expose faculty to research results for nonlecture pedagogy; provide stipends and grants for trying active learning.
- *What if our campus does not seem to have a shared culture or a common purpose?* Diversity and the unexpected are a boon for true learning communities.
- *How do you get faculty involved in developing student learning communities?* Find faculty who are willing to adopt new methods and those who are known for innovation in the classroom.
- *How do we decide which learning community model is best for us?* Assemble a faculty learning community to discuss possibilities, pros, and cons.
- *How do we plan for the development and implementation of learning communities?* Develop a team of selected faculty and staff led by a supportive faculty member or head of academic affairs.
- *What if faculty and staff believe learning communities will take too much time and energy?* Stress that improved student learning clearly outweighs the costs.
- *How can learning communities help high-risk students?* Develop a relevant theme, conduct workshops for students, and provide special support.
- *What is the most common shortcoming related to the best use of student learning communities?* When an institution is not a true learning organization, it tends to hew to the traditional.
- *What are the basic guidelines for student learning communities?* Guidelines developed by a study group should be based on institutional mission and culture.
- *What courses are best for student learning communities?* They work for classes of up to 20 to 25 students. Learning communities should involve intentional, scheduled activity outside the classroom.

- *What is an appropriate level of faculty involvement?* Faculty should receive information about learning communities and their specific goals and should meet periodically to determine the best way to relate course content and make learning more meaningful.
- *Where are the hard data supporting the value of student learning communities?* Longitudinal studies about persistence, learning outcomes, satisfaction, and other outcomes are the best source of data.
- *How should we publicize learning communities?* Attractive brochures, word of mouth from satisfied students, the institution's Web page, and press releases can get the word out.
- *What are the keys for maximizing the impact of residential learning communities, and what impact will they have on the present residence hall system?* Residential learning communities should be structured around common educational themes; they are particularly important for first-year students. The introduction of a different system, however, will require major efforts from residence hall staff.

CONTENTS

FOREWORD

Learning communities are one of the most commonly discussed concepts in higher education today. Studies on collaborative learning, community service learning, retention strategies, success for first-generation college students, women in science programs, enhancements for distance learning, first-year seminars, and redefining faculty roles and rewards all include some reference to learning communities. But although they are mentioned constantly, learning communities are not well understood or defined, and the term has different meanings for different people.

A review of the ERIC literature base in 1997 identified three distinct ways that the term "learning community" is being used. First, and most commonly, learning community refers to a curricular approach that links or clusters classes around an interdisciplinary theme and enrolls a common cohort of students. Second, in technology circles, learning community refers to a way to link students and faculty through the Internet. Third, in international circles, learning community describes linking people from different countries. Other definitions and uses exist as well. One of the valuable contributions of *The Powerful Potential of Learning Communities: Improving Education for the Future,* by Oscar T. Lenning and Larry H. Ebbers, is to provide an umbrella definition of and a framework for understanding learning communities.

Learning communities can be philosophically related to Deweyan principles—that education is most successful as a social process and is deeply rooted in our understanding of community and democracy. As we understand learning communities today, they evolved out of cooperative and collaborative learning movements that emphasized social interaction and active learning. Learning communities were almost always discussed in relation to the classroom. But what was once a pedagogical tool is now being used to transform all sorts of campus features, including classrooms, retention programs, distance learning, residential environments, and many other structures.

Why should anyone care about learning communities? Does this interest harken back to the experience in an Ivy League school or a small liberal arts college? Is a learning community really an alternative pedagogical tool that has become the panacea for all of higher education's woes? No. Learning communities provide a more specific but extremely valuable benefit. What we know from the research on teaching and learning is that learning communities use the best principles of student development. If learning communities also help to address other problems, such as diversity and the disintegrating sense of community on campus, so much the better. But be wary of those who see them as a panacea; learning communities alone will most likely not be the solution to these very complex problems.

Lenning, special assistant to the president of Bacone College and adjunct professor of higher education at Iowa State University, and Ebbers, professor of higher education and associate dean of the College of Education at Iowa State, provide a persuasive argument for the need for learning communities, citing such examples as Ernest Boyer's call for community on college campuses and Peter Senge's concept of the learning organization. Their definition of learning communities helps to clarify the various ways the term is being used. They break the term into four categories—learning organizations, faculty learning communities, student learning communities, and virtual learning communities.

The authors describe in detail the various types of student learning communities, the most prevalent form. Research on the benefits of learning communities suggests significant outcomes for students: higher academic achievement, increased retention, improved thinking and communication, greater understanding of self and others, and increased social effectiveness. They also describe the benefits to faculty—the breaking down of barriers that contribute to isolation, an increased sense of shared purpose, and greater curricular integration.

Finally, the authors provide a detailed map for individuals interested in creating learning communities. They gather principles from the literature on implementing learning organizations and on collaborative learning, and illuminate the principles with a case study from Iowa State University. They describe conditions that they found hinder implementation of learning communities, including the lack of shared values, resistance to the values of collaboration, lecturing as the predominant pedagogy, and lack of interest, time, and energy on the part of faculty. And they enumerate other conditions that assist in a smooth introduction to learning communities: having data available on the benefits of learning communities, developing a careful implementation plan that balances the involvement of faculty, developing basic guidelines and criteria, and choosing clear models and communicating the models effectively.

The Powerful Potential of Learning Communities builds
on earlier ASHE-ERIC publications that illustrate the benefits
of collaboration and community in learning: *Creating
Learning Centered Classrooms* (Stage et al.), *Academic
Controversy* (Johnson, Johnson, and Smith), *The Virtual
Campus* (Van Dusen), *Taking Teaching Seriously* (Paulsen
and Feldman), *Enhancing Student Learning* (Love and
Love), *Collaborative Peer Review* (Keig and Waggoner),
Faculty Collaboration (Austin and Baldwin), and *Cooperative
Learning* (Johnson, Johnson, and Smith). This collective
body of knowledge is critical for faculty and administrators
who are developing a framework for transforming institutions. Whether you are a faculty member considering the
integration of learning communities into the classroom, an
administrator contemplating integration in a department or
school, or an academic leader focusing on institutional
changes, *The Powerful Potential of Learning Communities*
offers helpful theoretical insights and practical advice for
moving your campus toward learning communities to increase learning for all students.

Adrianna J. Kezar
Series Editor,
Assistant Professor of Higher Education, and
Director, ERIC Clearinghouse on Higher Education

ACKNOWLEDGMENTS

The authors wish to thank many persons for their critiques and support of this publication. First, we want to thank Iowa State University for its support in many different ways. We particularly want to note the work of three ISU graduate students (now professional staff members): Lynnae Diefenbach, Laura Doering, and Stephanie Hamilton. Their early research projects were instrumental in helping us pull together much of the research on learning communities and to critique the drafts that were developed. In addition, we would like to thank John Schuh of Iowa State University, Steve Crow of the North Central Association of Colleges and Schools, Beverly Edwards of Fulton Teaching Resource Center, Jon Fife and Adrianna Kezar of the ERIC Clearinghouse on Higher Education, Louie Jackson, Marlene Smith, and Connie Spear of Bacone College, Bob Albrecht of Western Governors University, Bill Crothers of Roberts Wesleyan College, Frank Pfaff of St. Gregory's University, Bill Hamm of Waldorf College, attorney Denise Hill, the Reverend Chris Lenning, and the anonymous reviewers for their valuable suggestions. Special thanks are due Alisha Lenning, communications instructor at the University of Texas–Austin and at Austin Community College, who spent many hours editing the manuscript from the perspectives of faculty members at community colleges and universities. Jerlando F.L. Jackson, higher education graduate student at Iowa State, also provided important assistance during the later stages of refining the manuscript. And none of this effort would have been accomplished without the skilled technical work of Marva Ruther at Iowa State University.

Special thanks go also to Vincent Tinto at Syracuse University and Pat Terenzini at the National Center for Teaching, Learning, and Assessment at Penn State University. They were the original inspiration for our interest in learning communities and for beginning and sustaining the movement toward learning communities at Iowa State University.

Finally, no project of this nature is ever successful without the support of one's spouses, and Renie Lenning and Barbara Ebbers provided ongoing encouragement and understanding throughout this long process. They were invaluable in stimulating our thinking as they responded to various portions we had written.

LEARNING COMMUNITIES:
What Are They And Why Do We Need Them?

*Two are better than one, because they have a good re-
ward for their toil. For if they fall, one will lift up [the
other]; but woe to him who is alone when he falls and has
not another to lift him up. Again, if two lie together, they
[keep] warm; but how can one [keep] warm alone? And
though [one] might prevail against one who is alone, two
will withstand him. A threefold cord is not quickly broken.*
—Eccles. 4: 9–12, RSV
—(cited in Johnson, Johnson, and Smith 1991b)

This biblical passage reminds readers that community, where
people join in small groups to discuss, explore, and learn together, has existed for centuries as a central concept of learning. "The Talmud clearly states that to learn, one must have a
learning partner" (Johnson, Johnson, and Smith 1991b, p. 4),
and noteworthy proponents of learning through community
have existed for centuries: Quintilian in the first century, Lan-
caster and Bell in the 16th century, Comenius and the Common School Movement in the 17th century, Parker in the
19th century, and Dewey in the early 20th century. And a
creative new intentional approach to learning communities
can greatly improve learning for college students as we enter
the 21st century.

The Need for Learning Communities
Even at small liberal arts colleges, the predominant method
of teaching is still lecturing (Pascarella and Terenzini 1991).
The focus remains on teaching rather than learning, which
has an adverse effect on the amount and quality of intentional student learning. Moreover, "teaching is hardly ever
assessed in terms of . . . student learning and development"
(Astin 1993b, p. 421). Two primary challenges in higher education today are to meet the public's demand for maximizing
students' learning, and to be more accountable for what students learn. Everyone seems to agree—students, parents, employers, politicians among them—that undergraduate education in this country must improve dramatically.

In response to these pressures, regional accreditation
agencies mandated the creation of institutional assessment
plans to document and provide guidance for improving students' learning. But college and university faculty and administrators must develop a whole new paradigm for teaching
and learning to maximize learning for their undergraduate

students and to address the concerns of accreditation agencies. The availability of the Internet and new, user-friendly technologies resulting in a broad new array of distance learning programs across the country have introduced additional complexities that are of concern to the accreditation agencies and others. How can adequate student support services be ensured in remote locations? How does one ensure effective student-student and student-faculty virtual interaction?

Except in a few residential liberal arts colleges, "in postmodern society we have become so alienated and isolated from each other that we have had to artificially re-create the guise of 'learning communities'" (Wolfson 1995, p. 23). Students today are so busy with outside jobs, family care, and other activities that it is difficult for learning communities—which are necessary for the best learning—to form spontaneously. And because of the compartmentalization and departmentalization of collegiate life today (Masterson 1998), students often experience learning in an isolated, fragmented manner that also prevents needed learning communities from forming without outside assistance.

Fraternities and sororities could and should become the epitome of effective learning communities that promote students' learning. These entities have generally been just the opposite, however, because of their primary concern with socializing rather than learning and the alcohol abuse that often accompanies the socializing (Whipple 1998). Becoming effective "learning communities" could provide fraternities and sororities with an opportunity to develop a new, positive reputation emphasizing the maximization of learning for college students.

Although community colleges focus on teaching, their student retention rates are extremely low (Astin 1993a, 1993b; Pascarella and Terenzini 1991). Traditional students desiring bachelor's degrees, for example, drop out "at much higher rates than . . . expected [based on] abilities, aspirations, and family backgrounds" (Astin 1993b, p. 417).

And as for research universities, they are "so complex, so multifaceted, and often so fragmented that, short of a major crisis, they can rarely focus their attention on a single agenda. . . . The state of undergraduate education at research universities is such a crisis, an issue of such magnitude and volatility, that universities must galvanize themselves to respond" (Boyer Commission 1998, p. 37). The commission's report includes several recommendations:

1. Make research-based learning the standard;
2. Construct an inquiry-based first year;
3. Build on the freshman foundation;
4. Remove barriers to interdisciplinary education;
5. Link communication skills and coursework;
6. Use information technology creatively;
7. Culminate with a capstone experience;
8. Educate graduate students as apprentice teachers;
9. Change faculty reward systems; and
10. Cultivate a sense of community.

Although targeted at research universities, these 10 recommendations are equally valid at colleges specializing in undergraduate education, both large and small. With regard to recommendation number 10:

> *Research universities should foster a community of learners. Large universities must find ways to create a sense of place and to help students develop small communities within the larger whole. . . . The campus must be a purposeful place of learning in which every student feels special connections[, as] shared rituals play a powerful role in creating the larger university community in which smaller, personalized communities of learners can coalesce. . . . Commuters and residential students alike need to know that they are needed and valued members of the community* (Boyer Commission 1998, pp. 34–35).

This report sorts out the concept of community in this quotation and provides specific suggestions for creating special, purposeful learning communities that have the power to transform postsecondary education at all kinds of institutions by effectively promoting and optimizing students' learning. It also addresses all 10 of the commission's recommendations for reinventing undergraduate education. And while this report is targeted specifically to college and university faculty, staff, and administrators, and to local, state, and federal policy makers and planners, it also has important implications for elementary and secondary education.

"Community" as the Central Concept

"Community": It's everywhere! In thousands of geographical locations throughout the land, people gather in small, medium, and large groups (or dispersed associations) for some common purpose. We refer to towns, cities, counties, states, national regions, nations, continents, global regions, and the world—and their governing or other associational units—as "communities." So are any purposeful groups of people within and across these entities, including professional disciplinary associations, labor or trade unions, membership clubs, religious denominations, church parishes or congregations, synagogues, mosques, the audience of a particular television or radio network, station, or program, and Internet interchange networks. The list could go on and on.

People everywhere seem concerned about community development. A comprehensive database search at any major university library will reveal thousands of resources for "community development." Communities are multidimensional and amazingly diverse in size, composition, and other characteristics (Bellah, Madsen, Sullivan, Swidler, and Tipton 1985; Peck 1987; Sullivan 1994; R.L. Warren and Lyon 1988). "The United States is a nation of joiners. . . . Implicit in this penchant for 'getting involved' is the peculiarly American notion of the relationship between self and society. Individuals are expected to get involved—to choose for themselves to join social groups" (Bellah et al. 1985, p. 167).

The third college edition of *Webster's New World Dictionary* indicates that "common" and "fellowship" are root words for "community." Members of a community have something in common that ties them together for "companionship," "friendly association," or "a mutual sharing . . . of experience, activity, [or] interest." "In its richest sense, the word denotes something shared in common with others: common language, common ownership, common relationship, or common ideas. Of the many forms of the word 'common,' the concept of community is easily the most dynamic" (McEwan 1993, p. 4).

Although it is shared history and interaction or interplay among group members that bond them into a true community (Moss 1996), different observers have different views of what other specific primary components make a true, positive, healthy community that enables optimum learning to occur.

A community is a place where individuals "communicate honestly with each other," where their "relationships go deeper than their masks of composure," and where "openness to risk, an acceptance of human vulnerability, and the ability to live through community" exist (Peck 1987, p. 59).

True community involves inclusiveness, commitment, consensus that allows differences to be acknowledged and processed, contemplation, vulnerability, and "graceful fighting," where conflict is not avoided, minimized, or disregarded.

Generic characteristics of a community involve shared values, caring for one another, and appreciation of cooperation (Gardner 1990; Kouzes and Posner 1987). Communities are where individuals "discover unity, learning, and leadership" (Bennis 1993); they comprise individuals "who have come together and are committed to celebrating together, mourning together, and risking together" (Sullivan 1994, p. 15).

Members of a true, ideal community have enough confidence in themselves and other members of the community that surprise and the unexpected are welcomed and celebrated (Wheatley 1994). "I would be excited to encounter people delighted by surprises instead of the ones I now meet who are scared to death of them. Were we to become truly good scientists of our craft, we would seek out surprises, relishing the unpredictable when it decided to reveal itself" (pp. 142–43).

This description also implies trust. Community is not necessarily a static concept, and "as education and the world become more technology driven, the definition of community will change" (Wolfson 1995, p. 26). Frequently these days, writers and observers refer to the "global village"—or even an intergalactic community for the future, as did the writers of "Star Trek."

The Increased Focus on Community in Higher Education

The landmark report of more than a decade ago, *Involvement in Learning,* relates the American penchant for social involvement and interaction to one of its central recommendations, a call for colleges to focus on the involvement of students (Study Group 1984). Students' active engagement in learning processes enhances learning and leads to two fundamental principles:

1. *The amount of student learning and personal development associated with any educational program is directly proportional to the quality and quantity of student involvement in that program.*
2. *The effectiveness of any educational policy or practice is directly related to the capacity of that policy or practice to*

increase student involvement in learning (Study Group 1984, p. 19).

Moreover, such involvement leads to an important sense of community that facilitates learning and retention.

Over the past few years, higher education has been taken by storm with the word "community" and its variations, implications, and meanings. Broadly defined, "community," particularly "learning community," is not a new concept. Early accounts of undergraduate education focus on the value of learning within a community. Theorists like John Dewey and Alexander Meiklejohn were the forerunners of an idea whose time has arrived.

In 1987, the Carnegie Foundation lamented the loss of community and common purpose in higher education. Such expressions of concern, and the return to a focus on undergraduate education in the mid- to late 1980s, may have fueled our return to the community movement in our institutions of higher education.

> *There was widespread recognition that a larger, more integrated vision of community in higher education was required. This new vision should focus not on the length of time students spent on campus, but on the quality of the encounter. . . . It would relate not only to social activities, but also to the classroom* (A. Levine 1993, p. 326).

Boyer (1987) and his colleagues at the Carnegie Foundation found that 97 percent of college presidents felt the development of community was "very important" to the future of their campuses. The final report's six principles have served as a guide to our understanding of community in higher education (Boyer 1990, pp. 7–8; A. Levine 1993, p. 327):

- *By a* purposeful community, *we mean a place where faculty and students share academic goals and work together to strengthen teaching and learning on campus.*
- *By an* open community, *we mean a place where freedom of expression is uncompromisingly defended and where civility is powerfully affirmed.*
- *By a* just community, *we mean a place where the sacredness of each person is honored and where diversity is aggressively pursued.*

Theorists like John Dewey and Alexander Meiklejohn were the forerunners of an idea whose time has arrived.

- *By a* disciplined community, *we mean a place where individuals accept their obligations to the group and well-defined governance procedures guide behavior for the common good.*
- *By a* caring community, *we mean a place where the well-being of each member is sensitively supported and where service to others is encouraged.*
- *By a* celebrative community, *we mean a place where the heritage of the institution is remembered and where rituals affirming both tradition and change are widely shared.*

If we subscribe to the concept of community and individual ascendancy cycles (A. Levine 1980, 1993; A. Levine and Cureton 1998), then we are in the midst of a movement toward the community ascendancy cycle. We may, however, currently be in a period of discontinuity because of the rapid nature of change today (A. Levine and Cureton 1998). The current time is only the second time in history that such societal discontinuity has occurred:

There are rare times in the history of a society in which rapid and profound change occurs. The change is so broad and so deep that routine and ordinary cycles of readjustment cease. There is a sharp break between the old and the new. It is a time of discontinuity. In the history of this country, there have been two such break points.

The first was the Industrial Revolution, which began in earnest in the first decades of the 19th century. . . . The second break point or time of discontinuity is occurring now (A. Levine and Cureton 1998, pp. 151–52).

It is true not only on the part of students, but also on the part of colleges and universities.

Learning Communities in Higher Education

Many observers see community in higher education as an end as much as a means to an end, in the same vein as the "furniture of the mind" emphasized in the Yale Report of 1812. Community as a means is not unimportant, however, as indicated by Boyer's inclusion of "purposeful community" at the head of his list of six principles for understanding community in higher education. The focus of this report is strictly on community as an *intentional means to a particu-*

lar end, which end is to maximize learning of groups and individuals within those groups. By "learning community," we mean an intentionally developed community that will promote and maximize learning. For learning communities to be effective, they must emphasize active, focused involvement in learning and collaboration that stimulates and promotes the group's and group members' learning.

The leaders of the decade-old movement in this country involving learning communities for college students (referred to as "cross-curricular learning communities" in the next section) claim the term "learning community" should be limited to their particular models of organizing and working with undergraduate student groups to maximize learning. Common use of the term today is broader, however: "On the college campus today, the term *learning community* describes the environment that many institutions seek to create for their students, faculty, and staff" (Whipple and Sullivan 1998, p. 8).

Learning organizations have also been called learning communities (S. Ryan 1994). Moreover, the guru of the "learning organizations movement" used the term "learning community" in referring to those entities (see Kofman and Senge 1993, p. 5), as have more recent experts in this area (see Angelo 1997, p. 3). With regard to college students, the term "learning communities" in the past has been used to refer to collaborative/cooperative study groups (see Bouton and Garth 1983, p. 4). Finally, various recent works in the elementary/secondary education literature have used the term "learning communities" to refer to learning organizations as well as to various kinds of intentional student, faculty, and student/faculty groups to promote learning (see Baker and Moss 1996; R. Brown 1997; Cockrell 1996; Cusack 1995; Felner 1997; Fineman 1996; Gibbs 1994; Gutierrez and Stone 1997; Ishler and Vogel 1996; Krovetz 1993; Lenski 1996; Lieberman 1996; Lin 1995; Logan 1994/95; O'Neil 1995; Prawat 1996; Ravitz 1997; Rutledge 1996; Secules 1997; Shields 1996; Speck 1996; Trimble 1996; Weissglass 1996).

An examination of these various entities reveals that they have much in common that revolves around the concept of developing community to maximize learning. The conclusion therefore is that "learning communities" is legitimately the most appropriate generic umbrella term under which the more specific entities can be categorized. Although Boyer's six principles for understanding community in higher education may seem to have more implications for student life outside the classroom than in the classroom, they serve as a primary impetus for the emergence of "learning communities."

The term "learning community" is rooted in the traditions of the colonial colleges: "The first colleges in America were places that deliberately sought to create a community of scholars with common values. In those days, the focus on community and the moral character of students was as important a part of the college years as academic work" (Coye 1997, p. 25). Learning communities are also rooted in the ancient Greek ancestor of U.S. higher education. "From the early lyceums, to Emerson's 'circle of friends,' to my recent graduate seminar, education has always possessed special communities of learners for whom shared experience has special meaning" (McEwan 1993, p. 4).

The heritage of learning communities for students (see Gabelnick, MacGregor, Matthews, and Smith 1990) can be traced to experimental undergraduate colleges (Meiklejohn 1932; Tussman 1969). Experimental colleges, such as Eckerd College in Florida, those at the University of Wisconsin at Madison and at Green Bay, those at the University of California at Berkeley and at Santa Cruz, Evergreen State College in Washington, and New College at the University of Alabama, which became popular in the 1960s, used the concept of learning communities. So did the residential colleges modeled after the residential colleges at Harvard and Yale, which were in turn modeled after the residential colleges at Oxford and Cambridge (M. Ryan 1992), and the innovative residence hall programming to facilitate out-of-class learning that became popular during the 1960s.

It has been only since the late 1980s, however, that use of the term "learning communities" became prominent. Since that time, learning communities designed for both in-class and out-of-class student-student and student-faculty interaction began to evolve as a broad educational movement at the college level that came to be referred to as "the learning community movement in higher education." This national movement was spurred into being by, among other things, the Washington Center for Improving the Quality of Undergraduate Education, which through Ford Foundation and other funding supported the development of learning communities throughout the state of Washington, the publication of a Jossey-Bass New Directions source book on learning communities

(Gabelnick et al. 1990), and the development of a national clearinghouse on the topic through the financial support of the Fund for the Improvement of Postsecondary Education (FIPSE). The research studies on learning communities conducted by Vincent Tinto and his colleagues at the National Center on Postsecondary Teaching, Learning, and Assessment, a book about involving colleges (Kuh, Schuh, Whitt, and Associates 1991), and funding for development of learning communities provided by FIPSE provided further impetus.

Nearly all learning communities have "two things in common. One is *shared knowledge. . . . The second is shared knowing"* (Tinto 1998, p. 171, emphasis added). It is suggested that learning communities:

1. Incorporate and value diversity,
2. Share a culture,
3. Foster internal communication,
4. Promote caring, trust, and teamwork,
5. Involve maintenance processes and governance structures that encourage participation and sharing of leadership tasks,
6. Foster the development of young people, and
7. Have links with the outside world (Gardner 1989).

This review of the literature suggests that two dimensions of learning communities are important for higher education: *primary membership* and *primary form of interaction.* The first dimension differentiates characteristics the group members have in common. The second differentiates whether the group members have primarily direct, in-person physical interaction, virtual interaction, or nondirect interaction through written or other correspondence.

Three basic categories of learning communities within the primary membership dimension are important for higher education: (1) learning organizations; (2) faculty learning communities; and (3) student learning communities.

1. *Learning organizations* are colleges and universities "consciously structured to promote their own learning and that of their students and faculty members," as contrasted with what has generally been the case—"shared learning experiences" that seem "to promote individual, isolated, passive learning and forms of discourse that are

[currently] very much limited to the narrow boundaries of separate disciplines" (Tinto 1997b, p. 2).

2. *Faculty learning communities* are consciously and proactively structured faculty groups organized primarily to promote faculty learning.
3. *Student learning communities* are consciously and proactively structured student groups organized to promote student learning.

Some would contend that "alumni" is another basic membership category important for higher education. Although alumni are important in higher education and are a distinct group, alumni are concerned primarily about students' learning in their own alma maters, provide monetary and other resources to support such learning, and periodically gather for learning and other purposes as "former students." "Alumni" in this report are considered in the broad sense an extension and configuration of "student learning communities."

All three categories have in common the important characteristics discussed in the previous paragraphs. But readers should realize that although they are *distinctive,* the three basic primary membership types of learning communities important to higher education *are not mutually exclusive.* For example, the "educational communities of peace" (Knefelkamp 1992) to be built around the multicultural college curriculum could apply to any and all of the three categories. Similarly, student learning communities will usually also involve faculty.

The second dimension, that involving the primary form of interaction, also has three basic categories for characterizing any primary membership group (other dimension): (1) physical interaction, (2) virtual interaction, or (3) correspondent interaction.

1. *Physical interaction* pertains to any primary membership learning community where within-community communication or interaction is mostly direct, on site, and in person.
2. *Virtual interaction* pertains to any primary membership learning community where within-community communication or interaction is indirect in terms of physical place and location but direct in terms of time and effect through interactive computer, voice, and video networks.
3. *Correspondent interaction* pertains to any primary membership learning community where within-community

communication or interaction is largely indirect in terms of place and time, and occurs through letters, newsletters, radio or television broadcasts, and so on. Examples of this type of interaction include correspondence courses, book clubs, and "fan clubs."

Any category of one dimension can relate primarily to any category of another dimension. Therefore, in terms of within-group interaction, student learning communities can primarily involve and be categorized according to physical interaction, virtual interaction, or correspondent interaction. The two dimensions and their respective categories can be presented in a matrix as shown below, with the primary membership categories listed along the vertical axis and the primary form of interaction categories listed along the horizontal axis:

	Physical Interaction	**Virtual Interaction**	**Correspondent Interaction**
Learning Organizations			
Faculty Learning Communities			
Student Learning Communities			

Scope and Organization of This Study

This section has focused on "community" and "learning community" as overarching concepts in a new approach to collegiate organization and instruction. If implemented effectively and systemwide, this new approach will dramatically improve education in the 21st century.

The next section describes the different types of site-based student learning communities identified in the "student learning communities" category of the primary membership dimension of the typology, and "The Benefits of Student Learning Communities" documents the benefits to students and faculty that result from effective site-based student learning communities. The research makes dramatically clear that both students and faculty receive many important benefits from various site-based student learning communities. "Creating and Implementing Optimal College Student

Learning Communities" provides practical and applied information from the literature. And the last section discusses developments and directions for learning communities of the future. The primary focus is on learning organizations, faculty learning communities, and virtual learning communities. These topics are growing, but not yet well developed, segments of the literature on education learning communities. They will become increasingly important topics for analysis, discussion, and application. The section also includes some discussion of needs for comparative assessment and evaluation of the outcomes achieved with different site-based student learning community models.

TYPES OF STUDENT LEARNING COMMUNITIES

We . . . decided to use the term learning groups *as a general rubric, recognizing that a variety of labels are in use for such activity: cooperative learning, collaborative learning, collective learning, study circles, team learning, partner learning, study groups, peer support groups, work groups, learning community, self-help groups, and community education circles* (Bouton and Garth 1983, p. 4).

The first section discussed the concept and purposes of what we have called "learning communities." Because of the generic property of the terms "learning" and "community," we concluded that "learning communities" is legitimately the broadest, most generic term for the concept under study. The focus in this section is narrowed to one category of the primary membership dimension of "learning communities" that we called "student learning communities." This section discusses types of site-based student learning communities, or student learning communities that involve primarily physical, in-person interaction.

The student "learning community fosters social and intellectual involvement" and serves as a structure for "intellectual coherence and integration" (Stark and Lattuca 1997, p. 255). Models of student learning communities "assuredly result in more intellectual interactions between students and faculty, increased student involvement in learning, and higher levels of student motivation" (p. 256). Students learn from each other and from participating faculty, while faculty learn from students and one another. Student learning communities also serve as excellent vehicles for faculty development by bringing together faculty from different disciplines and providing a source of new energy and innovation in the classroom.

Student learning communities are relatively small groups of students (and faculty) working together to enhance students' learning and to help students become well-rounded, broad-based individuals. Most have some sort of faculty leadership and involvement. Generally, faculty organize them, but students are the predominant participants. Undergraduate students generally see little connection across the courses they are taking, even when skills emphasized in one course are needed in others. Well-conceived student learning communities are intended to combat this problem, and to help students perceive their cumulative education as part of the big picture of life. "Research shows that learning is most effective in a community where knowledge can be shared in class and out-side of class" (Jerry Gaff, cited in Collison 1993, p. A18). Thus, it becomes apparent that student learning communities that emphasize collaborative learning and serve both academic and social purposes will become important primary avenues for improving the education of undergraduate students.

The membership, format, linkages, and programming (curriculum and activities such as student journals, simulations, and collaborative learning) of student learning communities, in their most beneficial form, are purposefully designed to facilitate the maximum amount, mastery, effectiveness, and efficiency of learning. Members of an effective learning community interact to learn both inside and outside the classroom. Generally, each learning community includes study across academic disciplines. Members of a learning community may presumably interact in other modes as well, such as over the phone, through campus e-mail, a computer network such as the Internet, or distance learning using interactive video.

Learning communities, "by their very nature, juxtapose diverse perspectives and diverse disciplines so that teaching and learning inevitably engender social, cultural, and intellectual linkages" (Gabelnick et al. 1990, p. 121). In their most beneficial form, faculty carefully plan the membership, format, linkages, and programming for the learning community (R. Matthews 1994).

> *Learning communities are not merely block programming, an administrative convenience that facilitates registration and use of rooms. Rather, they are conscious intellectual structures that teachers create, and students participate in, to share a high-quality and enduring educational experience. . . . There are as many variations on the models of learning communities as there are institutions willing to participate. All, however, strive to provide an intense and supportive environment for intellectual growth and development* (p. 184).

Student learning communities are always intentionally organized to support more effective learning by students. The many different types can be grouped as follows:

1. *Curricular learning communities:* Cross-curricular learn-

ing communities; curricular cohort learning communities; curricular area learning communities
2. *Classroom learning communities:* Total-classroom learning communities; within-classroom learning communities
3. *Residential learning communities*
4. *Student-type learning communities.*

This section discusses all of these categories and subcategories. The categories are not mutually exclusive and can be
combined; for example, any of the curricular learning communities can include the students in a "residential learning
community" who are living and studying together.

Curricular Learning Communities
Cross-curricular learning communities
Before the early 1990s, a few collegiate institutions—particularly LaGuardia Community College, Temple University, Evergreen State College, the University of Washington, and community colleges throughout the state of Washington (B. Smith
1993)—focused on the design and development of special
learning communities. Since then, many colleges and universities—especially ones whose students are primarily commuters,
attend school part time, work full time, or have major family
responsibilities—have developed such learning communities.

Initially, the primary focus of such learning communities
(excluding federated learning communities, discussed later)
was to facilitate collaborative learning among entering undergraduate students (transfer students as well as first-year
students). Originally, this category was called "entering student learning communities," as the need to overcome inhibi-
tions and anxieties, and to develop meaningful community
that can facilitate adjustment to college and academic success is especially great for entering students. But as students
expressed desires to continue their learning communities
beyond the first semester, and even beyond the first year of
college, it became clear that such groupings can be valid
and meaningful at any time in students' careers.

Although some scholars (see Gabelnick et al. 1990) seem
to contend that these entities are the legitimate, only real
"learning communities," our study of the literature and our
deliberations lead us to call them "cross-curricular learning
communities," because they are in general cross-curricular
in nature. "Cross-curricular learning communities" is an im-

*... many col-
leges and
universities
—especially
ones whose
students are
primarily
commuters,
attend
school part
time, work
full time, or
have major
family re-
sponsibili-
ties—have
developed
such learn-
ing commu-
nities.*

portant subcategory of "curricular learning communities," which is a subcategory of "student learning communities," a category of "learning communities." An important aspect of developing such learning communities is to "purposely re-structure the curriculum to link together courses or course work so that students find greater coherence in what they are learning as well as increased intellectual interaction with faculty and fellow students" (Gabelnick et al. 1990, p. 5).

Formal college-level versions of such learning communities vary greatly in their purposes and the student populations they are designed to serve (R. Matthews, Smith, MacGregor, and Gabelnick 1997, pp. 462–65). The focus may be on fresh-man programs, general education, gateway courses, develop-mental and basic studies, honors programs, and/or work in students' major or minor.

In 1996, the Washington Center for Improving the Quality of Undergraduate Education published a directory of what we are calling "cross-curricular learning communities" (McLaughlin and MacGregor 1996). It identifies the following types of learning communities at 109 institutions in 26 states: (1) fresh-man interest groups, (2) linked courses, (3) course clusters, (4) federated learning communities, and (5) coordinated studies. Many variations of and approaches to each model are possible (B. Smith 1993). The Washington Center was founded to stim-ulate the formation of learning communities at colleges in the state of Washington. It currently supports and coordinates learning communities at 44 colleges and universities through-out Washington; it also acts as a national information clearing-house related to college student learning communities.

Instructors' receptivity to and preference for the learning community models vary according to their academic disci-pline (Gabelnick et al. 1990, p. 23; Stark and Lattuca 1997). For example, faculty in the sciences tend to use existing courses and sequences in the curriculum, and to prefer clus-ters, linked courses, and federated communities. Conversely, faculty in the humanities and social sciences tend to prefer integrated courses and synthesized new courses, and coordi-nated studies learning communities.

A review of other typologies for cross-curricular learning communities (Love and Tokuno *in press*) includes four possi-bilities. First is a condensation of an original five models (MacGregor, Smith, Matthews, and Gabelnick 1997) into three basic models: (1) student cohorts in larger classes, (2) paired or clustered classes, and (3) team-taught programs. Second is the typology of "common dimensions of successful learning communities," an expansion of a 1995 typology by Tokuno. Each learning community can be categorized into high-level, middle-level, or low-level positions along each of five dimensions: (1) student collaboration, (2) faculty collaboration, (3) curricular coordination, (4) shared setting, and (5) interactive pedagogy. The third possible typology is the degree of integration between any two dimensions in the second typology, for example, the degree to which courses are integrated along with the complexity of the collaboration that occurs. The fourth possible typology involves categories of learning communities designed for special populations, such as academically underprepared students, underrepresented groups, students with disabilities, honors students, residential students, and students with specific academic interests.

This review is limited to five models proposed by Gabelnick et al. (1990)—freshman interest groups, linked courses, course clusters, federated learning communities, and coordinated studies:

Freshman interest groups. The academic advising office at the University of Oregon originally conceived of the model based on freshman interest groups (FIGs), which allows interested incoming freshmen to choose from a list of special interests related to careers (e.g., prelaw), social issues (e.g., world hunger), and philosophy (e.g., what it means to be an educated person), among others. The students form small groups of 20 to 40, according to choice of topic, and take related courses as a group to fulfill their freshman course requirements. At Oregon, faculty who teach the selected courses are not expected to coordinate syllabi or co-plan courses during the semester, although they are invited to attend an initial group meeting to introduce themselves and their courses.

The FIG may have a common faculty adviser/mentor and/or an upper-class student peer adviser/mentor. The University of Oregon FIG program has a peer adviser for each group, who receives upper-division academic credit in leadership for his or her involvement (Gabelnick et al. 1990). The peer adviser "organizes the first FIG meeting during Orientation Week and then convenes the group weekly during the semester to explore issues and resources related to student life on campus, form study groups, or just spend some informal time together" (p. 24).

Linked courses. Linked courses are sets of courses that are in some way related to one another in terms of focus or content, as determined by faculty at the institution, and for which specific groups of students co-register. The faculty of the courses may or may not be expected to coordinate their course syllabi, assignments, and activities to achieve objectives for students, such as seeing the courses as an integrated and correlated set, applying what is learned in one course to the content and assignments in the other courses, studying the courses collaboratively in relationship to one another, completing common assignments across the courses, hearing common problems, themes, and concepts presented from diverse perspectives by the different instructors, and so on. What constitutes adequate cooperation, connection, linkage, and integration varies from instructor to instructor and among groups of instructors. Academic administrators may be involved also.

Students usually elect to participate in a learning community (from which they may opt out) and are then assigned to a specific group. Courses may be linked because they have common themes or issues, fit well into an interdisciplinary group, are required freshman or sophomore courses from different disciplines, and so on. Freshman (sometimes sophomore) courses in English composition, speech, history, humanities, social sciences, and science are commonly linked. In the well-known Interdisciplinary Writing Program at the University of Washington, in operation since the late 1970s, expository writing instructors cooperate with the instructors of 27 general education lecture courses in a variety of disciplines. Generally, about 20 students in a lecture course of 200 students are part of a linked writing course.

The writing course specifically develops thinking and writing skills in the disciplinary context, whether it be art, history, sociology, or biology. Usually the students in the smaller writing class make up only a small portion of the students in the larger lecture course, but they become a small community with a sense of identity and a shared, rigorous academic enterprise (Gabelnick et al. 1990, p. 20).

Different approaches to linked courses are possible. At a basic level, paired courses illustrate the variety of possibilities. A paired course is a course link made up of two courses, usually a skills course in combination with a content course. For example, (1) both courses share the same students and no other students are in either class, (2) both courses, say, composition and speech, are taught by the same instructor, (3) the two courses also enroll significant percentages of students who are outside the learning community (like the University of Washington example earlier), and (4) the two courses are combined into a linked course that enrolls twice the number of students and is team-taught by the two instructors.

Course clusters. Course clusters are a specialized version of linked courses. Twenty-five to 35 students, who constitute a learning community, enroll together (in the same section during the same term) in all three or four of the courses designated for that particular group of students. The instructors work together like those who teach linked courses. Students in the cluster may take courses outside the cluster in addition to those in the cluster, but the courses designated for the cluster constitute most of, if not all, the course load for the term. The faculty in this system teach courses both inside and outside the cluster.

This approach was initially implemented in 1978 at LaGuardia Community College in New York City (R. Matthews 1994; R. Matthews et al. 1997; Tinto and Love 1995), and it remains in operation on that campus. Each cluster consists of three or four courses, lasting one semester, based on a selected theme to tie the courses together. Instructors for the courses meet periodically and attempt to make the courses complement and support one another. Years after they were initially introduced, an integrating seminar of one credit was added to the course clusters. The college has separate, distinct course clusters for liberal arts students, business students, new students, students on public assistance, and more.

Federated learning communities. FLCs were created and implemented in the mid-1970s at the State University of New York–Stony Brook by philosophy professor Patrick Hill (1982) before he became provost at Evergreen State College. In the manner of FIGs, this model invites currently enrolled undergraduate students to volunteer to study together in groups of up to 40 a special set of three disciplinary courses. These "federated courses" relate directly to an overarching theme. In addition, however, the student group participates separately (no other students) in a specially prepared "program seminar" related to all three federated courses and taught by "Master Learners" from outside the disciplines of the federated courses. At Evergreen State College, Master Learners are relieved of normal teaching duties.

> *A key individual in the FLC model, the Master Learner is a faculty member from a discipline other than those of the federated courses. He or she is expected to become a learner with the students and to fulfill all the academic responsibilities of a student in each course. . . . But the Master Learner's age and training puts him or her in a unique position to assist students in discovering and exploring the integrative and opposing threads and points of view of the three courses* (Gabelnick et al. 1990, pp. 27–28).

Faculty teaching the federated courses also benefit from the Master Learner's presence in terms of learning how their courses are being used and understood. Because of the cost involved in having a Master Learner, some institutions have deleted this faculty position from the model. Some have one of the FLC instructors teach the seminar; others delete the integrative program seminar and use proxies for the Master Learners, such as selected/trained upper-division students.

Coordinated studies. In 1970, coordinated studies debuted as part of Evergreen State College's curricular design, a year-long learning community for first-year college students modeled after the groundbreaking approaches of Meiklejohn (1932) and Tussman (1969). "Coordinated studies" means that the students and faculty assigned to the learning community are involved together in a complete program of study that requires a collaborative learning focus by participating faculty. The size of these learning communities is proportionally larger than course clusters, generally involving groups of 60 to 100 students and three to five (commonly three) faculty members who teach only in the coordinated studies program. The number of faculty and the size of the total group depend on the number of courses involved. The faculty-to-student ratio in such a program is approximately 1:20; it may go to 1:25. Most coordinated studies last only one quarter or semester; the faculty involved and program offerings usually change each academic term.

Faculty and students all work together full time in active, interdisciplinary, thematic learning, but modes of delivery and emphasis on subject matter vary. Some coordinated studies programs are very specific in terms of content and skills and are highly sequenced; others are not sequenced or focused in terms of content and skills.

> *The full-time nature of coordinated studies breaks open the traditional class schedule with diverse possibilities for scheduling longer blocks of time for extended learning experiences. . . . Typical coordinated studies programs involve a mix of plenary sessions (lectures, films, or presentations) and small-group work (workshops, seminars, and lab sessions). "Book seminars" . . . are the hallmark of most coordinated studies programs. Seminars are extended group discussions of a primary text or article, usually held twice a week. Each faculty member convenes his or her seminar group of about 20 or 25 students and acts as a facilitator, encouraging students to develop skills in taking charge of seminar time to dissect the text* (Gabelnick et al. 1990, pp. 29–30).

Coordinated studies communities are highly complex and require much faculty energy over an extended period of time, but the highly integrative, intense experience provided is extremely valuable to students. Such communities also provide enormous opportunities for faculty to be creative.

Curricular cohort learning communities

Academic programs in which the same students are together in every course because they are required to take the same courses at the same time to complete the program on schedule (which some have called "lock-step programs") are called in this monograph "curricular cohort learning communities." If a student drops out of a module or course, he or she is generally required to wait until the next cycle (another class) comes along, probably because participating students are required to take the courses in sequence so the group's cohesiveness and support are not adversely affected. Such programs are more economically efficient than programs having elective courses from which each student can choose. In addition, they force students to be in one learning community for the entire duration of the program; if collaborative methods are integrated throughout, students' achievement and retention are potentially much greater.

Vocational programs at community colleges and many upper-division and graduate programs for adult learners (for example, St. Thomas University in Minnesota and Antioch) frequently use this method. Two undergraduate cohort learning communities, one for older and one for traditional-age students, are described in the following paragraphs.

This monograph's senior author, while vice president for academic affairs and academic dean at Roberts Wesleyan College, a small church-related four-year college in Rochester, New York, during the 1980s, oversaw the development, approval, and implementation of an upper-division accelerated bachelor's degree program in management of human resources (several years later renamed Organizational Management).

The program was designed for employed individuals over 25 years of age who had completed two years of lower-division work at a two-year college and had enough significant work experience and associated learning to earn an additional year of supporting coursework credit through assessment of a portfolio. Organizational Management was a year-long evening program consisting primarily of course modules in the major and application of what is learned in class to a significant year-long on-the-job project.

Once a group of 15 to 20 students had signed up for the program and been assessed and approved for enrollment, the program began, regardless of the time of year. The group was introduced to its lead instructor, who taught some of the program modules and served as the group's ongoing mentor for the entire year. Each lead instructor had the proper degree credentials, and was specially oriented and trained to work with individuals as well as an entire group in the role of adviser and supportive friend. Each group of students in the curricular program took all the modules together as one group in a specified order.

Because the student groups completed the program at various times during the year—almost always many weeks or months before commencement—a special graduation dinner with a follow-up recognition ceremony and program was arranged for each class upon completion of the program. Students' families, professors, and other available faculty and administrators from the college attended these events. As part of the program, the graduating students were always invited to share experiences and testimonials about the past year. Invariably, they talked about the positive and rewarding experience of studying together and socializing together inside and outside class, the helpful interaction with their lead instructor and other professors, and how the support from one another—and their instructors—had pulled them through and allowed them to succeed beyond their highest expectations.

An extremely effective learning community had developed for every class, and *no* students dropped out of the program. Each group of students and mentors/instructors developed a remarkable esprit de corps, and students' achievement and development of skills were superb. Employers noted how beneficial the program had proved to be for their employees. The program was subsequently purchased and implemented, over the next decade, by 50 colleges and universities across the country whose faculty tailored it to local needs.

Employers noted how beneficial the program had proved to be for their employees.

After eight years at Roberts Wesleyan, the author served for six years as executive vice president and dean for academic affairs at Waldorf College, a small, rural two-year college in Iowa. There he oversaw the development, approval, and preparation for full-scale implementation of two accelerated upper-division bachelor degree programs for traditional-age students: a two-track program in business (management and finance), and a two-track program in communications (electronic media and print media). The class schedule for both upper- and lower-division students was adjusted to allow a lower-division commencement in mid-April, allowing the first upper-division semester to take place in April through July. The final three semesters were to be completed before the end of July of the following year, approximately 15 months after the students completed their lower-division program.

These upper-division accelerated-degree programs included additional innovations, such as the ability to take only two courses at a time and only in the afternoon, and a semester at Oxford in England that involved taking two courses and doing an internship with a British company (in addition to internships in the United States). Esprit de corps, group support, and common mentors occurred for these traditional-age students, just as was true of older students in the Roberts Wesleyan program. Conversations with Waldorf faculty members and students involved in the program and with current Waldorf administrators confirm that similar effects on students' achievement, retention, and esprit de corps are being experienced among traditional-age college students, just as they were at Roberts Wesleyan.

1. As of July 1997, only one bachelor's program student had dropped out since the program began in spring 1994;
2. Of the 30 bachelor's degree students graduating in June 1997, 22 earned honors;
3. The graduates have been finding desirable employment and been successful on the job (Waldorf College 1997).

Because of its success with these two upper-division programs, Waldorf is now implementing additional curricular cohort accelerated upper-division programs. The college has also begun offering its upper-division business program in Phoenix, Arizona.

At both colleges, other institutional innovations and factors played an important role in the success of their respective accelerated-degree programs. Yet there can be no doubt that the learning community aspects of both programs were imperative to the programs' success. Moreover, dramatic increases in total enrollments, beyond these programs, occurred at both colleges in the years following implementation of their respective programs.

Curricular area learning communities
Throughout the history of disciplinary higher education, faculty, students, and alumni in each of the curricular disciplines have viewed themselves as part of a specialized profession that is seen by its members as a distinctive community of scholars. By the time undergraduate students are juniors and seniors majoring in a disciplinary area, they have many common courses with their disciplinary student peers and tend to begin seeing themselves as members of that disciplinary community. As a result, upper-division students tend to interact more with their disciplinary peers and faculty within their major than with other students and faculty.

The Association of American Colleges and Universities sponsored a series of studies on the college major (summarized in Schneider 1997). Although the studies found fragmentation, lack of coherence, and undue subspecialization in the major, and a resulting adverse impact on "involvement in human-scale learning communities," curricular area learning communities still have potential:

> *But why begin de novo to create learning communities within the academy? Departmental majors already bring together faculty members and students who share an interest in a constellation of related questions, interests, and approaches. If we accept the value of community as an important resource for students' intellectual growth and development, the role, work, and interrelationships among the departmentally based communities of interest that have already formed in higher education can be a promising place to begin* (Schneider 1997, p. 240).

If faculty in a disciplinary department intentionally organize their student majors into meaningful discussion and study groups that collaboratively facilitate learning and commitment to the values of the discipline, those student groups can become well-defined and effective learning communities. (It should be noted that disciplinary groups on many campuses that have intergroup interaction and discuss and share thoughts with one another currently do not meet the intentional faculty intervention criterion for being a bona fide "learning community.") Faculty who organize student departmental/disciplinary clubs can transform them into legitimate learning communities, usually not the case, if they provide and stimulate quality, targeted collaborative learning and fellowship experiences aimed at enhanced learning.

One model of a formal curricular area learning community emphasizes problem-based learning. Such groups are organized around discussing solutions for particular real-life problems within the discipline (Cordeiro and Campbell 1995; Woods 1996). Students deal in small groups with a problem they are likely to face as a professional. They need knowledge organized around problems rather than disciplines, and they are responsible, individually and as groups, for their own teaching and learning.

Another model of a formal curricular area learning community was developed at Drexel University. Drexel had officially approved redesigning its entire curriculum for freshmen and sophomores so it could implement an all-student focus on learning communities by curricular area, beginning with freshmen entering in fall 1996 (Collison 1993). "The idea of 'learning communities' in which students work in small groups and study in interdisciplinary programs is not new. [But] educators say Drexel is unique in its effort to adopt the approach universitywide" (Collison 1993, p. A18).

The results of a five-year pilot project in its College of Engineering, funded by a $2.1 million grant from the National Science Foundation, led to Drexel's decision. In the pilot undertaking, each group of approximately 100 engineering students was assigned to 10 to 12 professors and taught by that same team of professors over the first five terms of college. In the pilot project, students participating in the learning communities were exposed to more practical courses earlier in their college careers. Faculty reported they developed close relationships with, and really came to know, students by staying with the same students for five terms. Moreover, 89 percent of the learning community students (compared with 74 percent of those students *not* assigned to learning communities) were still engineering majors after two years.

Based on the results of the pilot project, the Drexel engineering faculty revamped the curriculum and adopted learning communities for *all* engineering students in fall 1994. All Drexel engineering students took expanded team-taught interdisciplinary courses (e.g., physics/chemistry/calculus), and the group of students also participated in a group engineering lab.

The university had approved a plan to implement this concept in all colleges of the university beginning in fall 1996 (Collison 1993). The engineering learning communities are institutionalized collegewide and continue to work well, but the Biology Department is apparently the only other academic department to implement the concept.

Classroom Learning Communities
Total-classroom learning communities
A classroom has often been viewed as a learning community in self-contained elementary schools where students and the teacher interact and work together continually and daily.

Generally, in classrooms where teachers work to effectively develop a sense of family, or community, across the classroom, all the students in the class view themselves as members of a distinctive learning community. Although a college class can similarly become a true learning community, it tends not to happen. The class meets only an hour several times a week, and lecturing remains the dominant mode of instruction (Pascarella and Terenzini 1991; Pollio 1984).

The data collected by the assessment techniques reported in Angelo and Cross (1993) can be aggregated for the class as a whole. The focus is on the class rather than on individuals in the class. The faculty member (a learner, too) can present the data to, and discuss the data with, the students in the class as a group. As group members reflect on the meaning of the data, they can become a powerful learning community (Angelo and Cross 1993). "Classroom research" is also important in a group's collaboration (Bruffee 1988).

One comprehensive K–12 model for developing classroom community—or a "total-classroom learning community"—that also is relevant for postsecondary education focuses on developing effective problem-solving and human relations skills in students, and on the instructor's becoming primarily a facilitator rather than the traditional teacher (Andersen 1995). This model emphasizes the "new R's" of reflection, responsibility, relationship, and respect and a philosophy of growth among students having three themes—experiential, developmental, and transcendental.

The experiential theme is the foundation out of which the other two themes emerge, but most models of teaching—such as those emphasizing knowledge, training, or acceptance of what is taught—are not concerned with what a student is experiencing. Real understanding comes only through experiencing something firsthand. The keys to success in experiencing are the quality of personal involvement, and the intimate involvement of the whole person in the learning event.

Five strands are woven into making the classroom a true learning community (Andersen 1995). The instructor should:

1. Implement the concept and practice of democracy;
2. Create a caring environment that responds to the real needs of students;
3. Master the art of facilitative process;

4. Use an innovative curriculum involving sequential and developmental activities that have meaning for the student; and

5. Act as an effective change agent.

An excellent example of a total-classroom learning community at the college level is the Phi Theta Kappa Leadership Development Studies course, a "great books" approach to leadership development created with a grant from the Kellogg Foundation as taught at Bacone College. Designed to assist students to develop their potential for leadership and to become productive leaders, the course is designed as a seminar, discussion, participatory model to enable students to become actively involved in the course's content. The course is limited to 20 to 25 students.

The course has 11 units: developing a personal leadership philosophy, articulating a vision, leading with goals, decision making, managing your time, team building, empowering and delegating, initiating change, managing conflict, applying ethics to leadership, and leading by serving. For each unit, a variety of techniques are used to engross students in the topic, which might include the use of readings, films, cases, small-group collaboration, and simulation exercises. At the opening session, the students get to know one another through conversations about who they are and how they need to improve, after which they each enter into an oral contract that what is said in class does not leave the classroom. Each student is required to keep a weekly journal about leadership activities they experienced or observed that were meaningful to them. They continually break into small groups of three or four for problem-solving, decision-making, and team-building group competitions; the membership of each group changes constantly.

One of the two team instructors for this three-credit course reports that, despite great diversity among students in terms of age, ethnic background, major, marital/family status, residential status, and so on, the total class (including the instructors) quickly evolves into a true, vibrant learning community with a unified desire to learn together how to become effective leaders. Moreover, the group shares a great deal of esprit de corps, excitement, and spirit of cooperation, and its members listen to and support one another. Group scores are always higher than the individual scores on competitive exercises.

Within-classroom learning communities

Formal models of cooperative and collaborative learning have focused on dividing students into groups of various kinds that we view as learning communities, and on implementing specified types of formats and group activities. Most within-class learning teams comprise four to six members and involve different roles for team members (often rotated), such as coordinator, recorder, and gatekeeper (Kagan 1989, 1992). For such within-class learning communities to be successful, the learning communities must be "cooperative learning groups" rather than "traditional learning groups" (Johnson and Johnson 1990). These categories can be differentiated as shown below:

Cooperative Learning Groups	Traditional Learning Groups
Positive interdependence	No interdependence
Individual accountability	No individual accountability
Heterogeneous membership	Homogeneous membership
Shared leadership	One appointed leader
Responsibility for each other	Responsibility only for self
Emphasis on task and maintenance	Emphasis on task only
Social skills taught	Social skills assumed or ignored
Teacher observes and intervenes	Teacher ignores groups
Group processing	No group processing

Practitioners of both cooperative and collaborative learning have advocated using cooperative learning groups, and most theorists/faculty practitioners consider these two basic forms of teaching part of the same thing. Although admitting some distinctions among the various entities, Davis (1993, p. 147), for example, equates cooperative learning with collective learning, peer teaching, peer learning, reciprocal learning, team learning, study circles, study groups, and work groups.

Some authors claim important distinctions exist between cooperative and collaborative learning, seeing cooperative learning as a broader concept, with collaborative learning a subset (K. Barr and Dailey 1996; Davidson 1990). Collaborative learning involves the shared creation of something new; cooperative learning involves learning together and supporting one another in learning, but not necessarily creating something new. Collaboration is "the process of shared creation: two or more individuals with complementary skills interacting to create a shared understanding that none had previously possessed" (K. Barr and Dailey 1996, p. 187).

Conversely, some see collaborative learning as the broader concept, with cooperative learning one subset representing "the most carefully structured end of the collaborative learning continuum" (B. Smith and MacGregor 1992, p. 12). Other proposed subsets include problem-centered instruction (guided design, cases, simulations), writing groups, peer teaching (supplemental instruction, writing fellows, mathematics workshops), discussion groups and seminars, and learning communities.

Others hold a similar view but see cooperative learning and collaborative learning as two separate concepts that use similar processes but for different purposes (Bruffee 1987, 1993, 1995; J. Cooper, Mueck, McKinney, and Robinson 1991; J. Cooper and Robinson 1997a; Rockwood 1995a, 1995b; Romer and Whipple 1991). "Cooperative learning means noncompetitive learning, in which the reward structure encourages students to work together to accomplish a common end. [Collaborative learning] takes the students one step further, to a point where they must confront the issue of power and authority implicit in any form of learning, but usually ignored" (Romer and Whipple 1991, p. 66).

The term "collaborative learning" was coined and its basic concept defined in the 1950s and 1960s "by a group of British secondary school teachers and by a biologist studying British . . . medical education" (Bruffee 1984, p. 635). It did not originate in U.S. higher education circles. Cooperative and collaborative learning have different historical roots, with cooperative learning having been emphasized in grades K–12 and focusing on the teacher's role in the classroom (Brody 1995). Conversely, collaborative learning has been emphasized at colleges, and focuses on ways to structure productive and positive interdependence among students while at the same time holding individuals accountable for learning outcomes.

Basically we learn by explaining to others our way of challenging each other's biases and assumptions, then negotiating together new ways of perceiving, thinking, feeling, and expressing [them,] . . . creating contexts [that] purposely structure dialogue across disciplines and professions, not just within them (Brody 1995, pp. 137–38).

Cooperative learning and collaborative learning are complementary to, and can support, each other (Brody 1995). A definitive article underscores this position by pointing out the ignorance within each tradition about the other tradition, providing meaningful college-level examples of both approaches, discussing the many meaningful similarities and differences, and pointing to the ways in which both approaches can be used to support one another at the college level (R. Matthews, Cooper, Davidson, and Hawkes 1995). "The roots and history of each approach have yielded a rich and varied body of literature and wisdom of practice. . . . Within collaborative and cooperative learning . . . there are significant differences among adherents, while at the boundaries there is a good deal of overlap between the two" (p. 37).

When one divides a class into collaborative learning communities and works with them effectively, the important learning takes place in those within-class communities rather than in the class as a whole (Lee 1996). Organizing the classroom in this way "decenters the teacher and empowers students" (p. 2).

"Although much has been written about cooperative learning, little is aimed at the college level" (Johnson, Johnson, and Smith 1991b, p. xix). By 1990, college faculty members' interest in cooperative learning was growing, however (J. Cooper et al. 1991), and more than 50 cooperative approaches to learning appropriate for the college level have been identified (Wilson 1996). Moreover, since Johnson, Johnson, and Smith wrote their handbook for college professors on using cooperative learning (1991b), the use of this methodology has become widespread in higher education.

There are two distinct approaches to such group work:

1. *Engaging in complex instruction,* designed to teach high-level concepts and materials to *all* students in heterogeneous classrooms "to break the link between status and the rate of participation," that is, to weaken or eliminate problems with status; and
2. *Fostering a community of learners,* where groups of students "engage in collaborative research, . . . share their information and understandings through jigsaw . . . and other activities," and apply their learning to new, more difficult tasks, reported on in a public exhibition or performance (Shulman, Lotan, and Whitcomb 1995, pp.

17–19). ("Jigsaw" [Aronson, Blaney, Stephan, Sikes, and Snapp 1978] is described later in this subsection.)

The following paragraphs briefly describe a number of within-classroom groupings reported in the literature on cooperative learning that can be appropriately used in college classrooms (see, e.g., Brandt 1991; Gibbs 1994; Knight and Bohlmeyer 1990; Lyman, Foyle, and Azwell 1993; S. Sharan 1980; Slavin 1995). Methods that are inappropriate for college students are excluded.

Each approach leads to a different type of learning community in terms of organization and process, yet in all cases it is cooperative learning that helps create the learning community (Johnson, Johnson, and Holubec 1994). A collaborative learning study group developed for the college level, supplemental instruction, is added at the end.

Groups of four. The simplest of within-classroom groupings (defined originally by Burns 1981), groups of four involve merely having groups of four *randomly* selected individuals sit and work together on a common task. The instructor introduces the problem and task, answers any questions, and assists students if they cannot assist one another on the task. Formal goals for the group are not stressed, and individuals are not accountable for the group's achievement. The group could report to the class and/or turn in one group homework assignment (which should mean the instructor needs less time to correct papers).

Circles of learning. Sometimes called "learning together," this approach calls for arranging learning communities throughout the classroom (Johnson and Johnson 1975). Four elements are emphasized: (1) face-to-face student interaction in small groups; (2) "positive interdependence," that is, students working together toward a common goal; (3) accountability, that is, the requirement that individuals demonstrate mastery of the material; and (4) teaching students how to work together effectively in small groups and assessing how well their groups function in terms of the group's goals. Each group should have no more than six members, and must be arranged in a circle. The group works as a team to understand and complete homework, construct or develop a product (such as a composition or a group presentation), share ideas with one another, and help one another to find answers to questions or prepare for a test. The teacher is responsible for praising and rewarding the group and its members.

As refined for use in a college classroom (Johnson, Johnson, and Smith 1991b, pp. 57–79), this type of learning community involves the faculty member's using the jigsaw approach (described later) and peer editing. The faculty member can also arrange structured academic controversies, cooperative reading pairs, group class presentations, laboratory groups, and drill review pairs.

Student teams and achievement divisions. This approach promotes the use of learning community groups within the classroom in competition with one another (Slavin 1980, 1991a). The group or groups found to exhibit the most and/or highest-quality learning, as reported to the group and the instructor, receive appropriate rewards. The reward suggested for the elementary/secondary level is recognition in a class newsletter, although more tangible rewards may be given to successful groups and members. The college instructor will need to determine rewards appropriate for and valued by college students. Individuals' accountability to the group is reinforced by having each person's score on a quiz contribute to the team's score. Scores may be adjusted by improvement exhibited.

Jigsaw I, II, and III. In this approach, each member of the group brings knowledge about specific assigned research that group members integrate into a whole. Jigsaw I involves each member of the learning communities (called "learning groups") in the classroom having access to only a portion of the overall information for the lesson (Aronson et al. 1978). Each member's assignment is different from other team members' assignments. The group integrates the separate information from each member into a whole before the teacher teaches the whole to the entire class. Jigsaw I consists of six steps:

1. Assign students to cooperative groups. Distribute sets of materials divisible by the number of members in each group to the groups and instruct them that each member is assigned one part.
2. Assign preparation pairs across groups, where members of the different groups work together on the same as-

signed segment, become experts on that area, and decide individually how to best teach it to the other members of their respective groups.

3. Have students from the different groups who learned
the same material share plans and ideas on the best
ways to teach the material to others. Then they practice
on each other and revise the presentation.

4. Have all members in each cooperative group teach one
another their area of expertise.

5. Evaluate students' level of mastery of all materials, and
reward the groups achieving a prescribed level of mastery
(for example, through some type of formal recognition).

6. Have each group discuss one way each member helped
the group's members learn, and then come up with
three ways learning could be improved.

Jigsaw II involves competition among the within-
classroom learning communities, also called "learning teams"
(Slavin 1980). Incentives and rewards are provided for both
cooperative and individual performance; the process and
content are designed so each team member has an equal
chance to contribute to the team's score. Individual incentives are relevant because each team member is individually
accountable for his or her separate performance.

Jigsaw III adds a "cooperative test review" to Jigsaw II
(Kagan 1989) for the "home team" (Steinbrink and Stahl
1994), leading to four levels and six phases. The first three
levels and phases are the same: (1) Home teams meet and are
oriented; (2) all members of expert teams, comprising members from across the home teams, become common experts
across the team's area of expertise through cooperative study;
(3) home teams reconvene, during which each member is
required to teach his or her expertise to the other members of
the home team. Phase 4 is an interim period of one to several
weeks for informal review and individual practice tests. Phase
5 corresponds to Level 4; the home team reconvenes to undertake formal cooperative review for the final exam. During
Phase 6, all the individuals in the class take the final unit or
term exam. Individual scores provide individual accountability; these scores are summed to determine team scores.

Group investigation. Group investigation, or small-group
teaching, focuses on students' self-regulation of learning

activities (see S. Sharan, Bejano, Kussell, and Peley 1984; S. Sharan and Hertz-Lazarowitz 1980; S. Sharan and Sharan 1976, 1992; Y. Sharan and Sharan 1989–90). Group investigation incorporates cooperative group tasks and means; it is as well a set of goal incentives. Implementation involves six specific stages:

1. The instructor assigns the general topic, and the class discusses it to reach students' agreement on the subtopics to explore.
2. Each learning community receives one of the subtopics and discusses how to investigate it.
3. Students in each learning community work together to gather the data and information they agreed to for their subtopic.
4. Students in the learning community collaborate in analyzing, evaluating, and integrating the information they each gathered, and plan a group presentation on the subtopic for the class.
5. Each learning community makes its planned summary presentation to the entire class.
6. The instructor and the class evaluate the reports, presentations, and individual contributions, and the instructor provides group and individual recognition as appropriate.

Co-op co-op. This approach is similar to group investigation and generally involves the use of student teams and achievement divisions or Jigsaw II before the unit is begun (see Kagan 1985, 1989). To motivate students, it presumably builds on students' natural curiosity, intelligence, and desire to advance their understanding of themselves and the world and to communicate their knowledge to others. In Step 1, the instructor encourages all students in the class to discover and express their interests in a subject as stimulated by a set of readings, lectures, and/or exercises and experiences. Unless the students are already working in teams, Step 2 involves assigning all students to four- to five-member groups.

In Step 3, each group selects a main topic, with the instructor's assistance and support, and subdivides it into minitopics that will each provide one individual's contribution to the group's effort. Each group member researches his or her topic (Step 4) and then shares the information learned with the remainder of the group (Step 5). After all students in the

To motivate students, it presumably builds on students' natural curiosity, intelligence, and desire to advance their understanding of themselves and the world and to communicate their knowledge to others.

group have presented their findings, the group discusses those findings (Step 6) and incorporates them into a group presentation (Step 7) given to the whole class (Step 8). In Step 9, the instructor assesses the individual papers and presentations on the minitopics. Group members assess each student's individual work within the group, and the entire class discusses and assesses each group's presentation.

Teams/games/tournament. This approach is similar to student teams and achievement divisions except that it involves a component of individual competition (see Devries, Edwards, and Slavin 1978; Slavin 1991a). Students of the same ability compete one on one in formal tournaments, with each student representing his or her team and winning points for that team. In subsequent rounds, winners compete against winners, losers against losers. Quizzes and tests are administered to individual students, and results are used to assign individual student grades for the course.

Team-assisted individualization. In this approach to collaborative/cooperative learning, also called "team-accelerated instruction," all students work alone on assignments individualized to each participant (see Slavin 1985). Students are also assigned to a team, and team members use answer sheets to check one another's practice tests. Individual students are responsible for ensuring that their teammates are prepared to take the final unit test.

Students are required to seek help from teammates before seeking the instructor's help to encourage discussion and peer tutoring. Team scores consist of the average number of units covered in each four-week period and the average of the scores team members earn on the tests for the completed units. Therefore, this approach to learning emphasizes both individual and group accountability and rewards. When used at the elementary/secondary level, certificates are awarded for achievement of specified criteria. For use at the college level, grades may be enough, but awards or incentives appropriate for and of value to college students can be used.

Tribes learning communities. The concept of tribes was developed and refined over the last 25 years by a chemist who became more interested in the chemistry between people and their social systems (see Gibbs 1994). A grouping and cooperative learning process, it is designed for use at all educational levels but is being used throughout the United States and beyond almost entirely at the elementary/secondary level. Within a classroom, student peers are grouped into year-long tribes learning communities that vary in size from three for preschoolers to five or six for high school students or adults. (A school that has had its faculty and staff trained in the tribes methodology and practice by one of more than 400 available certified trainers is also called a "tribes learning community.")

Each tribe (tribes learning community) is selected to be balanced in terms of students' gender and other relevant factors; through specially designed strategies and processes, an ongoing, long-term tribal community results. Each tribal member learns to apply a set of collaborative skills and to value inclusion, caring, self-esteem, individual differences, attentive listening, community, goal setting, problem solving, assessment, celebration of achievements, and mutual respect, appreciation, support, and cooperation (see also Gibbs 1995).

Supplemental instruction. Supplemental instruction was developed in the early 1970s at the University of Missouri at Kansas City to help students in selected barrier courses form specially supported study groups meeting outside class for the duration of the course. Much empirical evidence suggests that supplemental instruction leads to greatly improved academic achievement and retention for the participating group (Martin and Arendale 1994).

Open to all students in the targeted course, supplemental instruction is announced at the first class session of the term and begins during the first week of classes, approximately six weeks before the first examination for most courses. Students' participation is voluntary; the sessions emphasize group interaction and mutual support for others in the group. Each student group is announced and led by a supplemental instruction leader, who is trained by and works under the guidance of the supplemental instruction supervisor, a trained professional staff person who oversees the program. Leaders are selected students who took the class previously and were successful. They are taught to be learning facilitators who integrate course content and study skills, and to provide useful feedback to the course's instructor. Many colleges and universities throughout the country now use supplemental instruction.

A new version of it developed at the University of Missouri at Kansas City, called video-based supplemental instruction, uses videotapes of professor's lectures (Martin and Blanc 1994).

Residential Learning Communities
In contrast to the structural linking of the disciplines (Gabelnick et al. 1990) and Astin's defining learning communities as functional group interactions providing integration within and between the curriculum and co-curriculum, some combine the structural and the functional (Schroeder and Hurst 1996). "Learning communities are characterized by associational groups of students and teachers [who share] common values and a common understanding of purpose, [and interact] within a context of curricular and extracurricular structures and functions that link traditional disciplines and co-curricular experiences in the vital pursuit of shared inquiry" (Schroeder and Hurst 1996, p. 178). It is clear that residence halls are an important part of the co-curriculum for residential students.

At many colleges and universities over the years, programming for residence halls and/or units within them has focused on the development of a learning community to support students' academic success. Community living in residence halls and programming for learning communities within them was often a primary factor explaining the superior academic performance and other important factors in skill development of residence students over commuter students (Schroeder and Hurst 1996). Conversely, many student fraternities and sororities have been primarily social in nature and have the reputation of not facilitating the academic success of their members.

According to one study, institutions stimulating the most fruitful involvement by their undergraduate students tended to be small, residential, and usually private colleges where involvement is expected (Kuh et al. 1991). Research over the years has demonstrated that resident students' learning and retention can be improved through programming that increases the quality and relevance of students' involvement in learning. Moreover, worthwhile proxies to involvement in learning-related residence halls (see Chickering 1974) can also be realized at commuter institutions.

Three major needs have been identified in response to the question of what this country needs from her colleges

(Wingspread Group 1993): attention to American values, reforms to increase educational achievement, and opportunities for life-long learning (Marchese 1994).

> *It would be hard to think of a better venue to pursue these goals in than the residence halls of America's colleges. . . . The chance to "go away to college" and take up studies in residence has always been a wonderful opportunity for students; today, it's a "best chance" for campus educators* (Marchese 1994, p. xi).

Despite such potential, the promise of residence halls for improving students' achievement has not been reached (Pascarella, Terenzini, and Blimling 1994). "We have become increasingly convinced that residence halls can make unique contributions to achieving the objectives of undergraduate education. We believe, however, that residence halls, as currently conceptualized and managed, are not realizing their full educational potential" (Marchese 1994, pp. xv–xvi). When confounding student factors such as scholastic ability are controlled, either statistically or experimentally, the evidence suggests that college students living in residence halls *do not* have better (or worse) study habits and practices or academic achievement than commuters—despite residence hall students' having clear statistical advantages over commuters (and increasingly so as college students get farther into their college careers) in many other important outcomes (such as social and extracurricular involvement with peers and faculty, satisfaction with college and its environment, commitment to the institution, persistence and graduation, ability to think critically, intellectual orientation, autonomy, academic and social self-concept and confidence, self-esteem and ego development, flexibility, aesthetic, cultural, and intellectual values, and social/political perspective).

But what form should improvements to resident students' learning take (and presumably that of fraternity and sorority members as well)? One suggestion is to transform college residence halls, and the groups of students who live there, into true learning communities with academic learning as a primary focus (Schroeder, Mable, and Associates 1994). The potential for increased learning is significant: Residents of college "living learning centers" in one study had significantly higher academic achievement, even after other relevant factors were controlled for, than residents of traditional residence halls (Pascarella, Terenzini, and Blimling 1994). They also achieved statistically higher levels than students in traditional residence halls on the other student outcomes listed in the previous paragraph. Students in traditional residence halls have, in turn, been found to surpass commuter students on these outcomes as well as in academic achievement.

The residential learning community developed at Auburn University during the 1970s is a good model for other institutions to emulate, as it models four essential principles for learning communities: involvement, investment, influence, and identity (Schroeder 1994). In addition to grouping students according to curricular major or intended career, as was done at Auburn, residential students can be grouped in other useful ways, such as multicultural learning communities structured around "multicultural and interracial themes" (Schroeder 1993), service-learning communities (Schroeder 1993), freshman-experience learning communities (Upcraft, Gardner, and Associates 1989), "values-inquiry" learning communities (Kirby 1991), and learning communities structured around "intentional democratic values" (Crookston 1980) or "empirical and symbolic modes of inquiry" (Shaw 1975). (See Anchors, Douglas, and Kasper 1993 and Schroeder 1993 for guidelines for making such residential learning communities maximally effective.)

Earlham, Stanford, Michigan State, and Maryland were found to be exemplary in their efforts to connect residence halls with the curriculum (Whitt and Nuss 1994a). Another review of integrated living and learning at residential colleges (T. Smith 1994) found two exemplary models: (1) the traditional, well-established, mature four-years-in-residence living/learning colleges at Yale University, which were begun with 10 such colleges in 1933 and expanded to 12 in 1962; and (2) the innovative, evolving four living/learning colleges developed at Northeast Missouri State University (now Truman State University) in 1988, each consisting of 60 percent freshmen, 25 percent sophomores, and 15 percent juniors and seniors.

A residential version of FIGs at the University of Missouri–Columbia allows as many as 20 first-time freshman students to take three courses together and live on the same floor in the residence halls with a peer adviser who is assigned to help the freshmen during their first semester of college (Univ. of Missouri 1997). Some of these residential FIGs include International House ("a global village on . . . campus"), the First-Time College Students Community ("a community of friendly support in a brand new world"), French and Spanish Language Houses ("a community where language skills are enhanced daily"), the Honors Residence ("a community of scholars"), the Fine Arts Residential College ("charged with creative energy"), Life Science Learning Community, Open for Business, Business and Computing, Leadership, Men in Engineering, and Women in Engineering. Students can remain in the Wakonse Learning Community Hall—"a collaborative project between departments . . . and approximately 100 university faculty who have shown a commitment to innovation in teaching and learning [where students] . . . are co-enrolled in a humanities sequence taught in the residence and participate in a variety of academic and co-curricular experiences, including service learning, career exploration, and subject mastery workshops"—throughout their undergraduate careers (Pike 1997, p. 4).

Two other current models of residential learning communities are exemplary. The first, the Living and Learning Together programs at the University of Maryland, focuses on the first two years of college, the second, Michigan Learning Communities at the University of Michigan, on all four years of undergraduate school.

The Scholars Program at the University of Maryland–College Park is a two-year residential program for academically gifted students. Open to commuters (10 percent of all participants) as well as living/learning center students, the program is designed to (1) "'make the big store small' without giving up the advantage of size," (2) encourage "students who share common intellectual interests to study together in courses organized around common themes and to live together in selected residence halls," (3) encourage "students and faculty to interact in informal settings on and off campus," (4) integrate the curricular and the extracurricular, and (5) create the environment of a small college within the larger university. Participants are grouped so they can take 14 to 17 credits of curricular theme courses together over the first two years of college that meet core graduation requirements. Themed clusters include advocates for children; American cultures; the arts; business, society, and the economy; environmental studies; life sciences; public leadership; science, discovery, and the universe; and science, technology, and society. Central to each cluster is a colloquium, "a movable feast of campus intellectual life [that] brings together students and leading members of the faculty to discuss both conventional wisdom and the newest discoveries." Faculty for the honors program take students on field trips and engage them in hands-on learning opportunities.

The living/learning communities at the University of Michigan include students through all four undergraduate years. The 360-student Lloyd Scholars Program, established in 1962, is open to first- and second-year students from any undergraduate school or college. Its residence hall has "thematic corridors for bringing students with similar interests together." Many of the program's instructors live in the residence hall, and courses are taught in classrooms in the residence hall. The Residential College Program, established in 1967, has its own faculty, and offers a variety of interdisciplinary and disciplinary concentrations and majors that feature small classes, provide special seminars, and involve a variety of informal intellectual and social gatherings among students and faculty. Residential learning communities established more recently include the 21st Century Program (requiring a time commitment of four to six hours per week and including the 21st Century Seminar, upper division student–taught mastery workshops, an option to take other courses with other 21st Century participants, and opportunities for community service), Women in Science and Engineering (which features academic advisers in the residence hall, formal study groups for selected courses, incentives to form informal study groups for other courses, short courses and workshops on academic and nonacademic topics, field tours, informal meetings with top administration officials, game nights, retreats, and team-building activities), the University Undergraduate Research Opportunity Program, and the Residential Honors Program. These programs have had a significant positive effect on achievement and retention, including progress toward eliminating the traditional gap between minorities and nonminorities on these variables (Dix 1996; Hummel 1997).

Student-Type Learning Communities

A typology of learning communities designed for special populations (Love and Tokuno *in press*) includes five categories that we call "student-type learning communities." They include learning communities for:

These programs have had a significant positive effect on achievement and retention, including progress toward eliminating the traditional gap between minorities and nonminorities on these variables.

- The academically underprepared, such as at LaGuardia and Leeward Community Colleges;
- Underrepresented groups, such as at Delta College and the University of Akron;
- Students with disabilities, such as at Leeward Community College;
- Honors students, such as at the University of Maryland; and
- Students with specific academic interests, such as at the University of Michigan.

Other possibilities are inclusive educational communities for minority students (Harris and Kayes 1996) or African-American students (Treisman 1985).

The assumption that students in general are homogeneous was once warranted in studies of the effects of college, but it is no longer because college students are becoming increasingly heterogeneous (Pascarella and Terenzini 1998). It is increasingly important to break students up into meaningful groupings by type to be able to assess the effects of college on students. Likewise, consideration should be given to "type" in the development of learning communities.

It is commonly acknowledged that students from the same background and/or with common student-type characteristics (for example, international students from the same country, region, or culture, students from the same race, rural students, urban students, students of the same gender, disabled students, students with the same learning style, and athletes) have historically tended to socialize and study together. In some cases, even Greek organizations have been considered specific types (Whipple 1998). Whether or not such groups facilitate students' learning depends on their orientation, goals, and approaches to learning. Frequently, the group's common interest in social activities distracts from effective joint study.

The literature on student development has created many of the foundations on which understanding of student types is based. These foundational theories as well as emerging theories (see Upcraft 1993, e.g.) may be used in creating specific student learning communities. Much of the work in studying students and students' learning began in the early 1960s (see, especially, Chickering 1969; Newcomb 1966; Sanford 1962), leading to various classifications of students—

for example, the widely publicized typology developed by Clark and Trow (1966)—and resulting in efforts to identify students "by groups."

During this time, the theories of moral reasoning and cognitive development (Kohlberg 1971 and Perry 1970, for example) that guide much of our current thinking about student type also became prominent (Upcraft 1993). These developments were followed by the development of the Myers-Briggs Type Inventory (Myers and McCaulley 1985), Kolb's Learning Styles Inventory (1985), and other assessment instruments designed to sort students into groups. All these developments were designed to enhance faculty and student affairs practitioners' understanding of students, their learning styles, and, specifically, the most effective methods of instruction. Classifications in the area of vocational interest (e.g., Holland 1966; Super 1957) helped provide additional focus on students' ability to learn and make choices.

Although many advances are being made in understanding students' learning styles, it is also important to consider the importance of gender and diversity in student-type learning communities. For example, undergraduate students are influenced more by the values and behavior of those of the same gender than those of the opposite gender (Astin 1993b).*

One of the most influential theories in creating student-type learning communities is involvement theory (Astin 1985), which posits that various kinds of students' involvement with students, faculty, staff, and the institution (even campus employment) contribute to positive student bonding, academic success, and retention. Not only has this theory had a major impact on approaches to students' learning, but it also has been the cornerstone of many institutional retention programs, leading to several areas of specific emphasis, including gender and race.

Much of the specific research regarding gender is focused on differences in gender in learning communities by institutional type, such as women's colleges and historically black colleges and universities. A study of the source of degrees among groups of women found that "special focused colleges" (student-type learning communities)—predominantly

---

*See Upcraft, Gardner, and Associates 1989 for an excellent review of resources on gender and diversity and Pascarella and Terenzini's National Study of Student Learning (1991). Work is continually emerging in this area, and Pascarella and Terenzini plan to update their book in the future.

white women's colleges, historically black women's colleges and coeducational institutions, and Spanish-serving institutions—graduate disproportionate numbers of women who earn a doctoral degree and are listed in Who's Who directories compared with white coeducational institutions (Wolf-Wendel 1998). It is important to allow students in these environments to grow and develop in institutions (learning communities) that are "safe, protected, supportive, [and] welcoming, and . . . where there are people around them who look like them" (p. 178). These findings speak directly to the need for creating special learning communities for women within predominantly white coeducational institutions.

Women in science and engineering programs are specific examples of the creation of such learning communities within an institution. Creating learning groups or learning communities within residence halls for such programs can help maintain focus and support for women science and engineering students. Colleges need to become more diligent in creating learning communities for these women that connect early introductory courses as well as specialized precollege learning communities for women considering science and engineering.

To help ensure the success of minority students, colleges should consider students' perspectives in creating learning communities that are based on ethnicity and that reduce the barriers to students' academic success (Padilla, Trevino, Gonzalez, and Trevino 1997). Cooperative learning (a component of learning communities) is a real strength within the American Indian culture and could lead to the development of strong programs for Native American students that focus on group learning (L. Brown and Robinson Kurpius 1997).

The complexity and interaction of all these forces continue to become more understandable. This increasing clarity, in turn, makes it even more evident that student-type learning communities require serious thought, exceptional planning, creativity, and evaluation—true of the other types of learning communities as well.

THE BENEFITS OF STUDENT
LEARNING COMMUNITIES

> *Student retention in learning communities is high be-*
> *cause students feel they are active participants in their*
> *education. They can confront each other, create mean-*
> *ing jointly with other students and faculty, and dis-*
> *cover and experience how group work deepens individ-*
> *ual insight [that] can translate into other community*
> *efforts, breaking down the idea of learning alone, being*
> *alone, teaching alone* (Gabelnick 1997, pp. 31–32).

The first large-scale attempt to implement and assess the effects of undergraduate student learning groups was initiated
in 1980 by the U.S. Fund for the Improvement of Postsecondary Education through the solicitation of proposals on active
learning. Upon reviewing dozens of project evaluation reports, FIPSE staff concluded that learning groups were the key
variable accounting for successful learning across all projects.

> *To start with, learning groups work—that is, they en-*
> *hance learning—irrespective of the type of institution,*
> *type of student, level of education, or subject matter.*
> *Indeed, learning groups promote the broad liberal edu-*
> *cation goals that are often more honored by educational*
> *rhetoric than pursued in classroom practice—specific*
> *information and content, general disciplinary concepts,*
> *generic cognitive abilities, interpersonal skills, knowledge*
> *about higher education communities, and understand-*
> *ing of how to learn. Learning groups seem to increase*
> *both the efficiency and effectiveness of learning. Learn-*
> *ing groups have also sparked many faculty . . . to re-*
> *assess their teaching* (Bouton and Garth 1983, p. 4).

This section discusses the effects of college student learning communities.

Benefits for College Students

The "involvement" model (Astin 1984, 1985, 1993a, 1993b)
and the "student departure" model (Tinto 1988, 1990, 1993,
1998) provide theoretical and conceptual reasons why student learning communities should impact college students
positively, and much research supports both models. The
models suggest that learning communities should increase
students' development, achievement, and persistence
through encouraging the integration of social and academic

---

lives within a college or university and its programs, and through quality interaction with peers, faculty members, and the campus environment. "A fuller appreciation of the potential of the peer group as a facilitator of the learning process could . . . serve to improve undergraduate education in *all* types of institutions" (Astin 1993b, p. 415).

A college's academic and social systems affect students' experiences inside *and* outside the classroom, with effects varying from campus to campus and from student to student (Tinto 1998). In one study, the effect of academic and social integration on persistence was more pronounced at four-year colleges than two-year colleges (Braxton, Sullivan, and Johnson 1997), "more likely the reflection of the varying academic and social attributes of institutions and the students they serve than of the underlying process of persistence" (Tinto 1998, p. 169).

Findings of related research

In general, people tend to remember only 10 percent of what they read, 20 percent of what they hear, 30 percent of what they see, 50 percent of what they hear *and* see, 70 percent of what they say, and 90 percent of what they say *and* do (Dale 1972). In a collaborative student learning community, where students teach one another, "saying and doing" is emphasized. Moreover, the one teaching is required to conceptualize, organize, and understand what is being taught (also true of peer teaching).

Students' interaction with others is important for large classes as well as small classes. For example, a study of students in large college classes and perceptions of factors contributing to their learning found that "other students" was the second most mentioned factor (Wulff, Nyquist, and Abott 1987).

Much documentary evidence suggests that active, focused, quality involvement by students with peers and faculty in the campus environment—inside and outside the classroom—can lead to much higher academic achievement, educational aspirations, maturity, self-understanding, and retention than otherwise (see, e.g., Astin 1993a, 1993b; Endo and Harpel 1982; Franklin et al. 1995; Kuh 1994, 1996a, 1996b; Lamport 1993; Pascarella 1980; Pascarella and Terenzini 1977, 1991; Springer, Terenzini, Pascarella, and Nora 1995; Terenzini and Pascarella 1994; Terenzini, Pascarella, and Blimling 1996; Whitt and Nuss 1994b). It is especially true when the focus is on "ideas and intellectual matters" (Terenzini and Pascarella 1994, p. 31), and commitment and loyalty to the institution and commitment to one's studies improve. Astin (1993a), however, expressed regret that large and impersonal commuter universities and community colleges became the norm for undergraduate students after World War II and over the years have educated increasingly larger percentages of undergraduate students in the United States.

Other research has found that differences in students' gender are related to the effect of involvement on academic achievement, persistence, and so on (Astin 1993b; Astin, Korn, and Green 1987; Pascarella and Terenzini 1979, 1983; Springer et al. 1995; Tinto 1993). Interaction between peers of the same sex appears to have the most positive effect on such student outcomes, with social relationships and values having a more important relationship to learning for women than for men.

A "college's effects on student learning are holistic, and . . . learning is shaped both separately and jointly by formal classroom experiences and out-of-class ones. . . . Researchers should more closely examine the multiple and interrelated sources of influence on any educational outcome" (Springer et al. 1995, p. 6). Learning communities can presumably contribute in and out of class to factors research has shown to be related to positive student change, e.g., the normative (group expectation) influence of faculty and peers in the community and, to a lesser extent, the modeling they provide (Bank, Slavings, and Biddle 1990; Tinto and Love 1993, 1994), the academic base the learning community provides (Terenzini and Wright 1987), and integration of coursework (Pascarella and Terenzini 1991).

Findings of the research on the outcomes of college student learning communities

Well-designed learning communities emphasizing collaborative learning result in improved GPA, retention, and satisfaction for undergraduate students (see, e.g., Gabelnick et al. 1990; MacGregor 1991; R. Matthews 1986, 1996b; R. Matthews et al. 1997; B. Smith 1991; Tokuno 1993). Moreover, learning communities of various kinds and in different institutional contexts that emphasize collaborative teaching and learning help undergraduate students—older as well as younger, remedial, regular, and honors, commuter as well as residential—in various ways (Cox 1993; Gamson 1994; J. Levine and Tompkins 1996; J. Lucas and Mott 1996; McCuen et al. 1996; MacKay 1996; Magid 1988; Pike 1997; Pike, Schroeder, and

Well-designed learning communities emphasizing collaborative learning result in improved GPA, retention, and satisfaction for undergraduate students.

Berry 1997; Tinto 1998; Tinto and Love 1993, 1994, 1995; Tinto, Love, and Russo 1994; Tinto, Russo, and Kadel 1994):

- GPA and the number of students on academic probation;
- Amount and quality of learning;
- Validation (Rendon 1994) of learning;
- Retention;
- Academic skills;
- Self-esteem;
- Satisfaction with the institution, involvement in college, and educational experiences;
- Increased opportunity to write and speak;
- Greater engagement in learning;
- The ability to meet academic and social needs;
- Greater intellectual richness;
- Intellectual empowerment;
- More complex thinking, a more complex world view, and a greater openness to ideas different from one's own;
- Increased quality and quantity of learning;
- The ability to bridge academic and social environments; and
- Improved involvement and connectedness within the social and the academic realms.

"Learning communities enhance the quality of campus life, contribute to the development of connections beyond the college, and help prepare students for the challenge of leadership" (R. Matthews 1994, p. 181).

These results reflect different types of college student learning communities and all types of students. It is important to remember, however, that some find participation in a learning community more valuable to some types of students than to others (Tinto 1998). Specifically, it is more valuable to commuting students and "students whose 'life tasks' make going to college difficult at best" (p. 172). And one study found that homogeneous student groups in residence halls by academic major at Harvard University had a stronger positive effect on persistence and other student outcomes for science students than for students in the humanities and social sciences (Light 1990). A study at Temple University, unlike other studies, found retention rates for students in the control group to be as high as those for FIG learning communities, although learning community students did earn significantly higher grades and had fewer course withdrawals and incompletes than the control group (J. Levine and Tompkins 1996). The second finding suggests that if retention for the two groups were compared later than at the end of the first semester, retention among learning community students would be significantly higher (that is, fewer students would drop out). Learning communities may also have some motivational value (Caprio 1993), a hypothesis deserving future investigation.

The effects of student learning communities can be very dramatic for groups employing effective collaborative methods. For example, a semester-long peer-assisted learning program involving collaborative study groups at American River College attained an 87.7 percent to 54.8 percent success rate over traditional classrooms in 1994–95, and an 86.6 percent to 55.2 percent advantage in 1995–96 (McCuen et al. 1996). Retention was also significantly better for students in the collaborative study groups. In both cases, English placement test scores (the control variable used) were not significantly different for participating and nonparticipating students.

A study of learning communities at William Rainey Harper Community College used carefully defined control groups and sophisticated methodologies (J. Lucas and Mott 1996). It is unclear whether the "holistic learning environments" of their learning communities had any impact on traditional measures of learning, but large improvements over their control groups were found on seven measures of attitudes toward learning and on many self-reported measures of students' group skills.

The study found that students' improvements were significantly greater for "coordinated studies" groups compared with "linked classes" groups, which fits with a finding of a research study supported by the National Center for Teaching, Learning, and Assessment (see Tinto and Love 1994, 1995; Tinto, Love, and Russo 1994; Tinto and Russo 1994). Although the study was not designed to compare the effects of different cross-curricular learning models, the authors found that their coordinated studies groups showed more positive change than their "course clusters" groups, which in turn showed more positive change than their freshman interest groups. Although we do not have complete assurance that the different models were implemented with equal effectiveness or that the student groups were comparable on all potentially relevant variables, the results suggest that well-done, more concentrated, longer-term approaches to learning communities that involve faculty as active, intentional participants are more effective than others. It could further be hypothesized that combining any of these cross-curricular learning community models with an effectively implemented residential learning community would add to the positive results obtained.

Another study of the effects of college learning communities on students (Pike 1997), even though it involved students at only one university and students' self-selection into the groups being compared, should be reviewed. The focus was on residential learning communities and involved a sophisticated study design built around the theoretical model of why residential learning communities affect students' learning. The model suggests that three entities interacting directly with the characteristics students bring to college lead to gains in their learning: (1) frequency and quality of opportunities for students' *involvement* in out-of-class educational activities; (2) frequency and quality of opportunities for intellectual *interaction* with faculty and peers; and (3) frequency and quality of *integration* between diverse curricular and co-curricular experiences. The model also posits that background characteristics directly affect the learning gained and the amount of students' involvement, interaction, and integration taking place (which affect the amount of learning gained).

This study compared results for students in residential learning communities and traditional residence hall first-year students at the University of Missouri during the 1995–96 academic year. All participating students were administered the College Student Experiences Questionnaire (Pike 1997); CSEQ scales were used to create measures of students' involvement, amount and breadth of students' intellectual interaction with faculty, amount and breadth of students' intellectual interaction with peers, and integration of curricular and extracurricular activities. CSEQ scales were also used to create two outcome variables, "gains in general education" and "gains in intellectual development." Background characteristics examined included gender, minority status, ACT composite score, and high school rank.

Analysis of variance was used to relate involvement, interaction, integration, and gains for the two groups of students, after which a two-group path analysis involving chi-square fits was conducted to differentiate the effects of all variables on the two groups. The findings revealed that, for all types of students, students in residence hall learning communities had significantly higher levels than did students in traditional residence halls on involvement, amount and quality of intellectual interaction with faculty and peers, integration of in-class and out-of-class information, and gains in both learning and intellectual development. These effects were direct for involvement and interaction, and indirect (through the in-volvement and interaction engendered) for integration and gains in student learning and intellectual development.

Tinto and Love's study (1995) also deserves special men-tion, because it involved a diverse community college in a large city with "exemplary" learning communities, was care-fully designed, and focused on using effective collaboration within the learning communities. Conducted at LaGuardia Community College in New York City, it was one of three studies of first-year college students conducted by the Na-tional Center for Postsecondary Teaching, Learning, and As-sessment's Project on Collaborative Learning. (The other two studies were conducted at Seattle Central Community Col-lege, focusing on its Coordinated Studies Program, and at the University of Washington, focusing on its FIG Program.)

To be chosen for the study, the institution had to be similar to many others around the nation, and its learning communi-ties programs had to have been institutionalized for a number of years, serve a diverse group of entering first-year students, and involve the range of collaborative learning practices in place at colleges across the county. The purpose of the study was to come to an understanding of how different collabora-tive learning programs shape students' learning and persis-tence in postsecondary education:

> . . . to understand not only what students experienced, but also how those experiences were associated over time with their behaviors and changing views of learning and their subsequent persistence in higher education. . . . The study was not intended to determine to what degree the programs were achieving their intended goals and in what manner they could be more effective in doing so. While comparative information was obtained on the experiences, behaviors, and persistence outcomes of a comparison group of students, that information was used to understand programs, not judge them (Tinto and Love 1995, pp. 3–4).

At the time of the study, the college offered several learning community programs, each one targeted to a different group of students (developmental, vocational, liberal arts, and honors, for example), which students selected themselves. Learning communities included FIGs, coordinated studies, and other types. Twelve learning community classes and 16 traditional comparison classes were selected for the study. Quantitative (longitudinal surveys) and qualitative (observations and interviews of participants) methods were used for the study. Analysis of the data involved descriptive statistics, discriminant analysis, and multiple regression analysis. Because the professors in both learning community and control group classes had been trained and were experienced in innovative/collaborative teaching, the authors concluded that the findings understate the differences to be found in community colleges in general.

Although students in the learning communities had lower high school grade averages, they were more likely to aspire to a bachelor's degree, needed less time to complete their associate's degree, were less actively involved in using the library, had more positive views about the college and the various aspects of its environment, including the faculty, other students, their classes, and the campus climate, earned higher college grades, experienced higher continuation rates to four-year colleges, reported that it was easier to learn and that learning was more fun, had greater appreciation of diversity, had greater awareness of the connections between different courses, and preferred learning communities. Socially and educationally disadvantaged students in the learning communities had significantly higher persistence in college than socially and educationally disadvantaged students in the control groups. For the more academically able students, however, the two groups had similar persistence rates, possibly because abler students tend to in general have a strong desire to transfer to four-year colleges.

Benefits for Faculty

Research indicates that students are not the only ones who benefit from learning communities. Faculty members also benefit from organizing and participating in learning communities in several ways:

- Learning communities allow faculty to work together more closely and effectively.
- Learning communities lead to increased continuity and integration in the curriculum.

- Learning communities constitute a valuable activity for faculty development.
- Learning communities help participating faculty to view their disciplines in a more revealing light.
- Learning communities encourage faculty to share knowledge with one another.
- Participation in learning communities broadens faculty members' knowledge about pedagogy.
- Learning communities promote collaborative, active teaching.
- Participation in learning communities tends to increase collegial trust.
- Faculty generally find their work with learning communities satisfying.
- Faculty appreciate the results of learning communities on the amount and quality of students' learning, students' enjoyment of learning, and students' values and satisfaction.
- "The act of creating and participating in a learning community is itself a community-building event . . . breaking down the isolation of faculty and the essential loneliness of teaching as currently conceived and executed" (R. Matthews 1994, pp. 186–87; see also Finley 1990; J. Lucas and Mott 1996; MacKay 1996; Tinto 1998).

Faculty involved in establishing and working with student learning community programs for high-risk students at Long Beach City Community College perceived the key benefits to be the satisfaction of seeing students so engaged and actively involved in learning, the broadening of their own knowledge through connection and interaction with instructors in different areas, and the discovery that, rather than distrust colleagues, instructors can learn to count on their colleagues for suggestions and solutions (MacKay 1996).

Student learning communities can bring faculty together from across the disciplines and lead to faculty members' energy and innovation in the classroom (Stark and Lattuca 1997). In fact, one male faculty member reported, "My wife kept saying, 'You've got to teach this way again; you're a different person this quarter'" (R. Matthews 1994, p. 187).

Findings from Studies of Collaborative and Cooperative Learning

Hundreds of studies of collaborative and cooperative learning in elementary and secondary schools have been conducted over the years, including a meta-analysis of 122 studies (Johnson et al. 1981) and an analysis of 46 studies (Slavin 1983a, 1983b). A review and summary of the results of more than 375 studies over the previous 90 years, including some conducted at the college level, compared the relative impacts on academic achievement of cooperative, individualistic, and competitive learning approaches (Johnson and Johnson 1994b; see also Johnson, Johnson, and Smith 1991b for a comprehensive summary of findings related to using collaborative learning for college students, and Qin, Johnson, and Johnson 1995 for a more recent synthesis of research in this area).

These analyses found that collaborative and cooperative learning results in a variety of positive outcomes for students: academic achievement, a higher retention rate, increased critical thinking, higher-level thinking skills and strategies, motivation to achieve, self-esteem and confidence, trust in others, low levels of anxiety and stress, creativity, frequent new ideas, the ability to generalize to new situations, problem-solving ability, a commitment to learning, instructional satisfaction, positive attitudes toward the major or discipline, positive attitudes toward the institution, positive attitudes toward other students, a commitment to and caring for other students, positive perceptions of the instructor, less absenteeism and tardiness, feelings of responsibility for completing assignments, a willingness to take on difficult tasks, persistence in completing tasks, better listening skills, respect for others' perceptions and attitudes, a commitment to peers' growth, social skills, and social support. Others would add increased acceptance of different races and ethnic groups (S. Sharan 1994; Shulman, Lotan, and Whitcomb 1995; Slavin 1980).

Although most of the research in this area has been on elementary and secondary students, an increasing number of recent studies indicate the same findings apply to college students (e.g., Chase 1991; J. Cooper et al. 1991; M. Cooper 1995; Courtney, Courtney, and Nicholson 1994; Freemyer et al. 1995; Johnson, Johnson, and Smith 1998; McCuen et al. 1996; Price 1995; Purdom and Kromrey 1995; Robinson and Cooper 1995; Roychoudhury and Roth 1992; Springer, Stanne, and Donovan 1997; Wilson 1996).

Cooperative groups also promote students' involvement in college academic and social life (Brosnan and Ralley 1995; Pisani 1994), which leads to personal and social development

(Astin 1993b; Friedlander and MacDougall 1991; Glover and Hull-Toye 1995) and career attainment (Fischer 1995). The superiority of cooperative and collaborative instruction over traditional instruction can be quite significant; for example, the course success rate averaged 26 percent higher across disciplines for cooperative and collaborative instruction compared with traditional instruction for the Beacon College peer-assisted learning project, which involved semester-long collaborative study groups in math and science, at American River College (McCuen et al. 1996).

These findings are true for adults as well as for traditional-age college students (Simpson 1995), for at-risk students (Tyler 1993) and learning-disabled students (Gore 1993), for large, medium, and small classes (M. Cooper 1995; Cottle and Hart 1996), and for classrooms that are heterogeneous in terms of students' academic and linguistic ability and in students' ethnic backgrounds (E. Cohen 1994a). Although the findings have also been found to be true for gifted students, sometimes these students feel that an undue burden is placed on them to assist less able students. Some gifted students may also feel frustrated with the group's inadequate processing skills, lack of participation, and some members' personal problems (M. Matthews 1992; Schumm 1993).

Not all studies of college-level cooperative and collaborative learning showed increases in students' learning and retention over that obtained with traditional instruction. Even in those studies, however, most students reported they liked such instruction better than traditional instruction, and *none* of the studies found higher learning and retention for traditional instruction. When data suggest no discernible impact on students' achievement, such as that found in the study of collaborative learning at Kansas City Community College (Wilson 1996), accurate interpretation is often impossible. Such findings may result from ineffective collaborative methods, measures that are not sensitive, or a variety of possible flaws in the study's design and interpretation.

A recent meta-analysis of 128 studies about the effects of cooperative learning at colleges found positive results in all student areas (Johnson, Johnson, and Smith 1998). Although some college-level findings suggest some forms of cooperative and collaborative instruction are more effective than others, no clear pattern of "winners" and "losers" exists. This area is an important one for study.

Several findings of studies of collaborative and cooperative instruction relate to how the group's educational experience is organized. Academic achievement is facilitated by cooperative learning only if there is a cooperative task structure (groups working together and group rewards), cooperative incentives, and accountability for individual learners (Slavin 1983a, 1983b). A meta-analysis of previous studies found "cooperative goal structures that do not create intergroup competition produce greater achievement than cooperative structures that do create intergroup competition" (Johnson and Johnson 1994b). Group work was most beneficial for learning concepts, problem solving, and deep understanding of subject matter and content (Shulman, Lotan, and Whitcomb 1995). And group work has the greatest impact on linguistic problem-solving tasks when there is more than one legitimate solution (Qin, Johnson, and Johnson 1995).

Concluding Remarks

The benefits for students of collaborative and cooperative learning are similar to the benefits of college-level student learning communities. It is clear that well-designed and -crafted cooperative and collaborative learning experiences within learning communities—as well as the existence and makeup of the learning communities themselves—greatly benefit both college students and faculty. Moreover, the benefits for both groups are many and varied, and are often highly integrated into a perception of strong learning outcomes.

*It is a sad paradox that the institutions most clearly
dedicated to helping adult learners to learn are such
slow learners themselves* (May 1994, p. 45).

"Research shows that learning is most effective in a community where knowledge can be shared in class and outside of class" (Jerry Gaff, cited in Collison 1993, p. A18). Learning communities that emphasize collaborative learning and that serve both academic and social purposes for students will become a primary avenue for improving the education of undergraduate students, with effective collaborative learning crucial. "Collaborative experiences provide lessons that no lectures or homilies can provide. Asking students to share the responsibility for each other's learning teaches students their learning and that of their peers are inextricably intertwined and that, regardless of race, class, gender, or background, their academic interests are the same" (Tinto 1998, p. 173).

Collaborative learning involves two or more individuals who are actively engaged, working together, and challenging one another in ways that lead to mutually negotiated and created cross-disciplinary and/or new understanding, perceiving, thinking, feeling, and communicating (K. Barr and Dailey 1996; Brody 1995). But how can we maximize its quality? "However structured, collaborative learning strategies share common threads, not the least of which is students are expected to work together and become active participants in the classroom. In this way, all collaborative learning strategies emphasize the development of student learning communities and their importance to the learning process" (Tinto and Love 1995, pp. 2–3).

For dramatic student outcomes to occur, learning communities must be effective in helping students engage in active learning: "Rich, rigorous learning environments, active participation on the part of both students and faculty, and a sense of community make a positive, often profound difference in fostering student success" (R. Matthews et al. 1997, p. 457).

Every learning community should thus be designed and carried out in a manner that will maximize *both* active and collaborative learning, two areas that are not mutually exclusive and supplement and support one another. Both need to be effectively designed and executed. (And poorly designed cooperative and collaborative experiences can lead to worse results than traditional approaches [Johnson, Johnson, and

For dramatic student outcomes to occur, learning communities must be effective in helping students engage in active learning ...

Smith 1991a].) This section summarizes specific suggestions for accomplishing this task based on the literature and the authors' own analysis.

Active Learning

Active learning and collaborative learning are keys to optimizing the effectiveness and positive impact of education on members of student learning communities. Although collaborative learning always involves active learning, intentional active learning can, and often does, also take place outside collaborative learning.

Practical suggestions for developing, promoting, and implementing active learning in college students are provided in several sources (see Bonwell and Eison 1991, Bonwell and Sutherland 1996, and Meyers and Jones 1993 for excellent summaries of the research on active learning). Students themselves may be a greater obstacle to active learning than faculty members' commonly hypothesized reluctance to reduce their reliance on lectures, because, in one study, they averaged five hours or less of homework per week, had experienced primarily teacher-directed learning in high school, and were indifferent to learning (R.G. Warren 1997). Students need help to change their notions of workload (preparation ahead of class as well as before exams) and initiative (taking responsibility for learning facts on one's own so that time in class can be used for more valuable activities):

> *Colleges have to help students . . . appreciate that some of the most valuable learning must come from their own teaching. Fortunately, there is a lot of research pointing to the value of student effort. . . . Minimal student initiative associated with successful active learning requires preparing prior to each class, talking in class even if shy, seriously listening to the comments of fellow students, solving problems, and learning to live with ambiguity instead of oversimplified answers to complex questions. It also includes time management to accommodate a sizable workload, dealing with student "freeloaders" on learning teams, and overcoming peer pressure* (R.G. Warren 1997, p. 17).

Most research has found that active strategies positively affect students' learning *and* retention (Astin 1993b). In a factor analysis, Astin found that one factor called "active learning" included the following measures (listed in the order of loading): cooperative learning, presentations by students, group projects, experiential learning/field studies, students' evaluations of each other's work, independent projects, student-selected topics for course content, class discussion, minimal use of the lecture format, and student-developed activities (pp. 38–39). In this study, however, the active learning factor had a negative effect on students' retention, even though giving presentations in class, taking essay exams, and working on independent projects had a positive effect on retention and learning (pp. 196–97). Just because active learning techniques are used does not ensure success. Those techniques must be well designed and include a focus and content that are relevant (in students' eyes) to what is being learned. Otherwise, students will see such activities as superficial and not pertinent.

Suggestions from the Literature on Collaborative And Cooperative Learning

To design and maintain the most effective classroom-based learning communities for college students, we need to generalize observations from studies of collaborative and cooperative learning. But "successful use of groupwork requires much more than simply putting students in groups" (Shulman, Lotan, and Whitcomb 1995, p. 5). It is crucial for groups to be trained and organized to practice active and collaborative/cooperative learning.

Cases and group work

Using case studies involving problems, issues, or dilemmas can be useful in applications of cooperative and collaborative learning.

> Cases are candid, highly readable accounts of teaching events or series of events. They show a problem-based snapshot of an on-the-job [or other real-life] dilemma. Read alone, cases offer vicarious experience of walking in another's shoes. In group discussion, they are especially powerful, allowing differing points of view to be aired and examined. For that reason, cases are consciously designed to provoke discussion that is engaging, demanding, and intellectually exciting. . . . But cases are not simply narrative descriptions of events. To call

*something a case is to make a theoretical claim—that it
is a case of something, or an instance of a larger class.
. . . To be valuable as a case . . . the narrative should be
representative of a class or type of dilemma, problem, or
quandary that arises with some frequency in teaching
situations. Most rich cases, however, are cases of many
things. Cases may also be exemplars of principles, de-
scribing by their detail a general pattern or practice*
(Shulman, Lotan, and Whitcomb 1995, pp. 8–9).

Case-based teaching—such as commonly found in business, law, and medicine—should be the norm in education
and in other areas (see also Colbert, Desberg, and Trimble
1996; Hutchings 1993; Merseth 1991, 1995; Shulman 1992;
Silverman, Welty, and Lyon 1992; Sykes and Bird 1992).

Student groups
In addition to training student learning groups to function
effectively, faculty members must have clear-cut objectives
for each group that are understood by all group members
(C. Hunter 1996). Moreover, a student's learning style is an
important variable (Price 1994, 1995). In one study, visually
oriented college students needed visual and manipulative
materials in a lab setting to learn successfully as individuals
and a group in an anatomy and physiology course and a
beginning general biology course. (See Billson 1994 for 17
principles for effective interaction within, and eight criteria
for assessing functional effectiveness of, small groups that
apply to all college student groups.)

Some useful, practical insights come from work with "base
learning groups" of four or five college students working
together in class for one entire semester (Wheeler 1995). A
student leader should be *assigned* for each group; it does not
work to have the group members decide among themselves
who the group leader should be. Moreover, the instructor
should have several goals for all groups: have a peer support
group in the class; have the best students assist in the motivation and teaching of the poorer students; and use peer
pressure to motivate students to work harder. Certain group
tasks are especially useful, including semester projects, two-
minute questions, Jigsaw reading, and a group test followed
by individual tests (where the group test serves as a motivational review in preparation for the individual tests).

Other suggestions for implementing collaborative learning include introducing new activities slowly, avoiding selection of groups by students, seeking feedback from students, assigning roles in each group to ensure everyone's participation, preparing tasks for students who finish early, and establishing partners to complete homework (Orrange 1993). Although some insist that instructors should assign groups and leaders, others recommend that instructors allow students to choose their own (Carter 1995), suggesting group membership and selection of leaders should depend on one's knowledge of the students. (Our own experience suggests it is usually preferable for the professor to select the group members and leaders.)

If it is economically feasible, an effort should be made to train and financially reimburse student leaders for collaborative learning communities. As part of American River College's Beacon Project (1994) peer-assisted learning program, for example, faculty selected students who had successfully completed the course. They trained them in tutoring and collaborative techniques, and had them serve as learning assistants who worked six hours per week (three hours with their respective collaborative student groups, two hours in preparation, and one hour meeting with the faculty member). Both the collaborative student groups and the learning assistants showed positive results. (See Van Der Karr 1994 for a similar approach to first-year hurdle courses.)

The frustration with the lack of the group's processing skills (reported by some gifted students) and some group members' personal problems and lack of participation indicates that cooperative and collaborative learning is not for all students and that groups should be carefully planned and constructed. Moreover, effective orientation and training activities, and the integration of group processes into the program are very important.

How should nonparticipants be handled? Several tactics are possible to get these "parasites" (Carter 1995) involved: require each group member to bring written work to class in order to belong to the group, periodically give unannounced in-class assignments, and assign individual grades in addition to a grade for the group.

Other approaches
Some evidence suggests that students with negative attitudes toward reading and writing can be salvaged through the use of

small cooperative learning communities (Rose 1994). The key to their success is having small group partnerships with the instructor and reference librarians. Other creative approaches have been found to be potentially feasible or useful:

- Having college students teach selected topics to junior high school students to enhance learning at both levels (see G. Hunter 1994 for an application with biology students);
- Combining the principles of collaboration and continuous quality improvement/total quality management in teaching and testing students (Cooke 1994; Hansen 1993);
- Incorporating debate into collaborative activities and small groups to stimulate nontraditional first-generation composition students to formulate their own questions, problems, and hypotheses (Hess 1993);
- Integrating reading and collaborative learning into college writing courses (Sollisch 1988);
- Using role plays in which students are team players in business, using brainstorming, analysis, interviewing techniques, pricing analysis, effective communication, conflict resolution, and so on (Hudson 1995);
- Translating the six characteristics of "true community" (Peck 1987) into creative activities for building community in the classroom (Orbe 1995);
- Including structured activities where students make decisions on what to study, how to study it, and solutions.

The emphasis in all these suggestions is on "processing experiences" and understanding (Lander et al. 1995).

Resources for faculty

Although collaborative learning and cooperative learning have positive effects within student groups, they work in complex ways that cannot be reduced to a field manual (Tebo-Messina 1993). Nevertheless, many general how-to publications on effective collaborative and cooperative learning exist (see, e.g., Abrami, Chambers, Poulsen, DeSimone, d'Apollonia, and Howden 1995; Adams 1996; Austin and Baldwin 1991; Brandt 1991; C. Cohen 1995; E. Cohen 1994a, 1994b; Cramer 1994; Davidson 1990; Davidson and Worsham 1992; Gere 1987; Gibbs 1994; Hartley 1996; International Association 1991a, 1991b, 1992a, 1992b; Johnson and Johnson 1993, 1994a, 1994b; Kagan 1989, 1992; Kessler 1992; Kluge

1990; Male 1994; R. Matthews 1996a, 1996b; Putnam 1993; S. Sharan 1994; S. Sharan and Sharan 1992; Shulman, Lotan, and Whitcomb 1995; Slavin 1991b, 1995; Stahl 1994).

Other faculty resource books discuss and provide guidance about various collaborative activities that can contribute to more effective student collaboration and improved student learning from such collaboration (see, e.g., Morris 1993; Sego 1991). Activities include peer review, group problem solving, chalkboard problem solving, partner self-tests, group quizzes, the generation of questions by the group, group book reports, and team debates.

A number of additional publications focus exclusively on college students (see, e.g., Bosworth and Hamilton 1994; Bruffee 1993; J. Cooper and Robinson 1997b; Davis 1993; Gabelnick et al. 1990; Goodsell, Maher, Tinto, Smith, and MacGregor 1992; Hagelgans, Reynolds, Schwingendorf, Vidakovic, Dubinsky, Shahin, and Wimbish 1995; Johnson, Johnson, and Smith 1991b, 1998; Kadel and Keehner 1994; P. Love and Love 1995; McNeill and Bellamy 1995; R. Matthews 1996a, 1996b; Millis 1991, 1995, 1997; Nurrenbern 1995; Purdom and Kromrey 1995; Schoem 1993; Tiberius 1990; Wilson 1996 for detailed guidance on developing and conducting effective collaborative and cooperative learning activities for students).

A proposed developmental model for constructing collaborative learning environments also provides frameworks for the development of learning communities (S.J. Hamilton 1994). In the range of "teaching and learning contexts and accommodation to changing demographic and discipline-specific curricula, we have the basis for a developmental model for the construction of collaborative learning environments" (p. 93). After a review of different models of collaborative learning, a five-step model for the construction of collaborative learning environments is presented.

More than 50 cooperative learning strategies have been identified as appropriate for use with college students, all of them student centered and shifting the responsibility for learning from the teacher to the student (Wilson 1996; see also Kagan 1989, 1992 for in-depth and helpful details about most of these strategies).

An annotated bibliography of 99 studies pertinent to collaboration with college students also includes lists of 14 Web sites and seven networks or clearinghouses on college-level collaborative/cooperative learning (J. Cooper and Robinson 1997b).

More than 50 cooperative learning strategies have been identified as appropriate for use with college students, all of them student centered and shifting the responsibility for learning from the teacher to the student.

Another book includes practical material for college teachers that faculty in LEA/RN (Learning Enhancement Action/Resource Network) discussion groups at Iowa State University found stimulating and useful (Johnson, Johnson, and Smith 1991b).

Two books on collaborative learning from the National Center on Postsecondary Teaching, Learning, and Assessment (Goodsell et al. 1992; Kadel and Keehner 1994) also deserve special mention. The initial volume provides capsule summaries of specific collaborative learning programs at colleges and universities across the country, and identifies five collaborative learning networks available to interested practitioners. The second volume provides a large number of vignettes on general and disciplinary collaborative learning techniques and exercises—each of which includes a description, reported strengths, and reported difficulties—submitted by college faculty from across the country. Both volumes emphasize "how to," reproduce selected readings, provide annotated bibliographies, and share a variety of collaborative strategies that have been found to be successful in different college settings.

Faculty development

As indicated earlier, the case study approach can be used to train both experienced and inexperienced professors in using learning communities effectively (Shulman, Lotan, and Whitcomb 1995). Such training should focus on the importance of learning communities, the role of faculty, designing tasks that facilitate group work, motivating group members to collaborate, dealing with uncooperative members, assessment, and so on. The group's tasks must complement one another, demand individual contributions and participation from all group members, and result in maximum learning for all group members. Because using group work effectively is so different from traditional teaching, effective collaborative, cooperative learning methods, such as those described earlier, should be used to win over veteran faculty (Shulman, Lotan, and Whitcomb 1995). "Veterans discuss teaching situations that mirror their own, in the process reflecting on their values, attitudes, and assumptions and wrestling with the disequilibrium this creates. As a result, they often change their beliefs and teaching and learning and, thus, adopt very different ways of working with students" (p. 8).

Collaborative learning requires faculty to move from teacher-centered to learner-centered environments. Faculty must become proficient facilitators who can intervene effectively and provide support to students in such areas as learning content, the self-directed group process, completion of tasks, encouraging critical questioning, and developing effective critical-thinking, problem-solving, and decision-making skills (K. Barr and Dailey 1996). Successful groups share several characteristics: (1) goals and purposes that are clear to all; (2) straightforward communication that cannot be misinterpreted; (3) shared leadership within the groups; and (4) respect within the groups for the views of minority members (Carter 1995).

Such instructors must possess eight particular skills in facilitation to effectively support and cultivate group collaboration:

1. Refocus on issues when necessary to keep discussions from bogging down.
2. Validate and bridge topics to make the transition from one theme to another.
3. Use the group's energy to drive discussions.
4. Continually invite and encourage input and feedback.
5. Establish a cooperative group climate that fosters discussion.
6. Coach the students to draw out what individuals already know.
7. Teach and promote active, eyes-on listening.
8. Intervene proactively into conflicts among groups and students (K. Barr and Dailey 1996).

A study in a community college freshman teacher preparation seminar illustrates how the instructor's attitudes and assigned tasks are as important as any skills (C. Cohen 1995). Various factors contributed to creating a classroom "community of caring, interdependent, intrinsically motivated learners": "shared decision making, choice, and class meetings . . . ; a cross-cohort Student Advisory/Sunshine Committee . . . ; a teacher-student alliance . . . ; trained teams in cooperative learning techniques . . . ; and a class history through videos and photographs" (p. 57). The instructors also used a self-evaluation instrument called a "reflection rubric" and a checklist of social skills. Journal entries and interviews revealed that all the students felt empowered as a result of the course communications system.

Technology, including the use of cooperative multimedia, may play a more important role in collaborative learning in the future—beyond the current use of e-mail in some learning communities—in improving and supporting an increased, more productive sense of community in learning communities (Muhlhauser and Rudebusch 1994). Technology can contribute much to students' ability to work in groups, for example, learning-disabled students in mathematics classes (Rapp and Gittinger 1993), distance education (O'Malley and Scanlon 1989), electronically mediated project management (Fowell and Levy 1995), and collaborative work enhancement (Laws et al. 1995).

Problems, Pitfalls, and Responses: The ISU Case Study
The research literature demonstrates conclusively that well-designed and -implemented learning communities significantly and positively affect both students and faculty, but a commitment to learning communities cannot occur unless faculty buy in on their implementation.

The need to improve undergraduate student retention at Iowa State University

Iowa State University's "Strategic Plan for 1995–2000," approved April 1995, makes its "highest priority . . . to *improve the quality of undergraduate education* as measured by student retention, graduation, and placement rates" (p. 180). The strategic plan, which contains many items relating to the concept of learning communities, proposed significant increases in funding for this purpose over the five years.

Approximately 81 percent of ISU matriculating freshmen were still enrolled at the beginning of the second year, 72 percent at the beginning of the third year, and 66 percent at the beginning of the fourth year. Although these percentages compare favorably with state universities across the nation, each percentage point gain in retention would mean dozens of students' being positively affected. The effort would assist in ISU's goal to become preeminent among land-grant universities. Moreover, when student retention and graduation rates were aggregated according to various institutional categories, it became clear there was room for improvement, especially among certain segments of ISU's student population.

The beginning of learning communities at ISU
The ISU graduate program in higher education sponsored a visit by Vincent Tinto in fall 1994, during which he presented information about learning communities and related research

results to a number of key faculty and staff. The visit and presentations stimulated follow-up discussions about how learning communities could improve learning, retention, and satisfaction for students at ISU. Subsequently, the associate registrar, the director of the Center for Teaching Excellence, and the coordinator of the Orientation and Retention Program met with each undergraduate college of the university. These conversations led to agreements by each of those colleges to set up groups of students taking the same sections of courses (linked courses) throughout their first semester. In three of the colleges, some special collaborative programming was being developed that included involving Residence Life staff in special efforts to support learning communities.

Problems with implementation

The lack of ongoing financial support threatened the fruition and longevity of these beginning efforts. Particularly at risk was planning for steps needed to make the learning communities effective and productive, such as having faculty and staff orient students in how to be effective in learning communities, having faculty from different areas work collaboratively and cooperatively to make their courses dovetail, and designing exercises and problems for students to promote collaboration and maximize the benefits of learning communities throughout the semester.

By summer 1995, no such wide-scale organized planning had occurred because of constraints on time and energy. Several pockets of related activity occurred, but they were not enough for integrated, campuswide planning and assessment. Those involved in initiating learning communities at ISU for the fall semester of 1995–96 reported that they did not have time to focus on the long-term development and implementation of a well-designed and comprehensive assessment and evaluation plan for the project. They also felt that they lacked knowledge and expertise in both learning communities and their assessment and evaluation. In response, the director of ISU's Center for Teaching Excellence asked the chair of ISU's Professional Studies in Education Department for help, and the authors were assigned to develop a plan for implementation and assessment.

Another problem important at ISU—especially relevant for all research universities—related to promotion and tenure. Promotion and tenure at ISU continued to be based largely on productivity in scholarship and research, and faculty perceived that devoting major amounts of one's energy to teaching in learning communities could adversely affect one's scholarly productivity. Thus, until university administrators and rank/tenure committees are committed to giving significant credit toward promotion and tenure for involvement in learning communities, and until they recognize pedagogical research on innovations in and results of learning communities as legitimate scholarship, faculty in general will be reluctant to participate in such endeavors.

It became apparent at ISU that faculty incentives, such as financial support or release time or credit toward promotion and tenure, are crucial for the institutionalization of effective, ongoing learning communities.

Assessment of learning communities at ISU also had a difficult start, and it is still limited. Collection, analysis, and interpretation of data; dissemination of research results across campus and to other institutions; and provision of advisory input to departmental faculty and doctoral students for use in research studies must be major, ongoing activities.

Results at ISU so far

At an early point, the ISU higher education program developed a relationship with faculty and staff responsible for prebusiness students as the result of a graduate student's preparation for a master's thesis (Diefenbach 1996). Graduate students in the higher education program have conducted most of the research that has been done, although a formal assessment program is being developed. Preliminary evidence indicates that student retention has improved, as compared with similar groups of students not enrolled in a learning community. In addition, GPAs of students in learning communities are also higher when compared with similar groups not involved in learning communities. A special learning community project called BEST (Biology Education Success Teams) designed for high-risk students in biology did not improve retention significantly but improved freshman high-risk students' satisfaction enough so that the students requested and were granted permission to continue as a learning team for the next three academic years (see S.L. Hamilton 1997 for preliminary program results).

Based on the results of research at the University of California at Berkeley (Treisman 1985), it would be expected

that such high-risk first-year students would especially benefit from participation in learning communities because of
their traditional lack of support from academically oriented
peers. The same is true of first-generation college students,
as such students have been less involved with peers and
teachers in high school and are at high risk in terms of other
factors involving performance and persistence (Terenzini,
Springer, Yaeger, Pascarella, and Nora 1996).

Faculty learning communities have also become important
at ISU. Assistant dean of the College of Engineering Howard
Shapiro (now associate provost for undergraduate education)
became interested in student-centered learning designed to
develop higher-order thinking in secondary school students
while a member of the local school board. He and Barbara
Licklider of the College of Education (a specialist in collaborative learning) teamed up in 1994 to initiate and lead a faculty learning group of 14 members that met for two hours
every other week to discuss how to improve learning. They
studied student-centered approaches of various kinds, tailored them to their own needs, tried them out in their own
classes, and then reported back to the group.

The excitement generated within the group by the resulting improvement in students' learning, retention, self-esteem,
and higher-order thinking led to the development of a universitywide program called LEA/RN (Learning Enhancement
Action/Resource Network) to encourage the formation of
more such learning teams. By spring 1998, such groups were
meeting across campus, and 40 percent of all faculty in the
College of Engineering were participating in the program.

An article in the spring 1998 issue of *Marston Muses,* the
College of Engineering newsletter for alumni and friends,
illustrates the impact and potential impact of this program:

> *Associate Professor Doug Jacobson attended his first
> LEA/RN session in 1996. "I didn't realize at the time that
> this one meeting would forever change the way I teach,"
> he said. . . . Through various interactive exercises and
> group activities, he creates a safe environment for learn-
> ing. "Nothing is more powerful than having a room of
> 80 students in groups engaged. You can see and feel the
> learning taking place! . . . I've noticed higher test scores
> from the middle-range students and deeper understand-
> ing of the material. . . . Attendance rate is higher, in-*

class participation has increased, and there is a stronger positive attitude . . ." (pp. 1–2).

As indicated, various pockets of learning communities were being developed from 1994 through 1998, many of them in isolation from one another. An institution must provide significant central administrative support and coordination to the development and maintenance of student learning communities, but "the cost is easily offset by increases in retention, grade point average, and credits earned" (R. Matthews 1994, p. 182).

The ISU registrar and the assistant registrar served key roles in developing programs for 1997–98. They created special forms to help ISU faculty and others develop and coordinate learning teams. Doug Gruenewald, assistant director of residence halls, has been especially influential in the effort to improve learning communities at ISU. A learning community work group led by Corly Peterson Brooke, director of the Center for Teaching Excellence, has also been instrumental in the development of learning communities. Composed of faculty and student affairs staff, the work group developed a proposal for implementation that the president approved. In summer 1998, the effort at ISU was undergirded by a $1.5 million grant from the president to initiate a full-scale, coordinated, universitywide effort to improve, expand, promote, and assess ISU learning communities. The grant includes funds for a full-time learning communities support coordinator, a secretary, and a graduate assistant as deemed necessary to provide (1) needed faculty and staff training and consultation; (2) stimulation for various areas to share information and talk to one another on an ongoing basis about experiences with learning communities; (3) longitudinal campuswide stimulation and support for the development of innovative learning communities in the various departments and colleges, and advisory support for disciplinary research inquiry and dissemination within their areas; (4) carefully planned and carried out assessment, evaluation, and research to discover the ongoing effects of different approaches to learning communities and provide information for modification and refinement; (5) dissemination of findings to the higher education community through presentations at disciplinary conferences, monographs, and journal articles; (6) assistance to departments and colleges in developing and promoting grant proposals to outside agencies for funding the development of learning communities; and (7) help with educating the total campus community about what constitutes true educational quality.

Potential Problems and Solutions

This section addresses problems and questions that may be raised about learning communities, and proposes solutions for the problems.

• What if we have no campus-based learning communities and faculty are not interested in them?

Assemble a small group of faculty and student affairs staff to determine the feasibility of the idea for your campus. If appropriate, bring practitioners involved in learning communities at other campuses to your campus, or conduct visits to their campuses. Of utmost importance is the support of the president and provost or academic dean. Once the group decides learning communities are desirable for your campus, bring in a consultant/facilitator to help determine the appropriate model for your campus. No one model fits every institution, and many campuses have implemented several models from which students can choose. Start with the models discussed in this report that seem most stimulating or are of interest to faculty.

• What if lectures are the predominant method of teaching and active learning is not emphasized?

Most faculty members want the best for their students. Although they may be afraid of losing control of the classroom or not being perceived as an expert, or they do not understand collaborative and active methods of teaching, the group must start someplace. Therefore, it is crucial to begin with a small core of faculty volunteers who seem amenable and open to change.

Expose all faculty to the research results for nonlecture methods, and bring in an outside faculty member as a consultant who has effectively used and appreciates such student-oriented methods. Faculty trying these new methodologies and succeeding will tell other faculty. It is hoped that many of the other faculty will then begin to ask for support and assistance related to mastering the new methodologies. Another avenue is to provide instructional stipends or grants to try methods of active learning.

- **What if our campus does not seem to have a shared culture or a common purpose?**

Just because segmentation and diversity are true of one's campus does not mean the campus has no universal values or concerns upon which it can build a sense of community and a variety of student learning communities. For example, everyone presumably wants all students to have a quality, enjoyable, satisfying learning experience, so discussion on this topic could stimulate fruitful discussion about learning communities. Moreover, diversity and the unexpected are a boon for true learning communities. Begin by making a list of possible student groups that should be considered or discussed.

- **How do you get faculty involved in developing student learning communities?**

Find two types of faculty before participating in learning communities—known "early adopters" and those known for innovative classroom techniques. A reward structure for such innovation, such as credit toward promotion or tenure, financial incentive grants, release time to conduct such activities, or sponsorship from an outside group, might be necessary.

Resistance to change can be anticipated from traditional faculty, which is why it is desirable that the development of learning communities be initiated by faculty. Specific actions are required of faculty: (1) They must accept new "cognitive value-based frameworks" and new definitions of teaching and learning; and (2) they must practice new teaching methods in which the teacher is no longer the authority (J. Lucas and Mott 1996). They will be concerned that inordinate amounts of their time and energy will be required, that course content will suffer, that course content will not be as generalizable to other contexts or covered sufficiently, that the students will not be as well prepared for the traditional courses that follow, and that it will be more difficult to measure students' achievement and to assign grades for the course. In addition, they will be uncomfortable with the notion that students and teachers are mutual partners in learning and in evaluating students' academic progress.

As with any educational innovation being considered or implemented, sensitivity to such fears from faculty and care-

Resistance to change can be anticipated from traditional faculty, which is why it is desirable that the development of learning communities be initiated by faculty.

ful use of effective strategies for change are crucial for successful implementation of learning communities. The change must not occur too fast. "As instructors begin to change their mental models, there are typical reactions to the disequilibrium that they feel . . . (1) incorrectly communicated information and rumors; (2) polarization of faculty; (3) undermining loyalties; and (4) increased ambiguity about the project" (J. Lucas and Mott 1996, p. 8).

A major issue for faculty, particularly at large research universities, is the involvement of untenured faculty in the development of learning communities. If learning teams or learning communities are to be successful, the institution must intentionally include participation in those activities in the reward structure. This will be the most difficult part of the process, as faculty will disagree about how to reward this activity. At institutions where the reward structure is a problem, the student affairs division may have to take the lead. Another avenue may be to convince senior faculty to initiate the activity, but no matter what else you do, senior faculty should be informed and involved in decisions at an early point.

- **We are overwhelmed by the many models and cannot decide which are best for us.**
Begin by forming a faculty learning community to discuss possibilities, and their pros and cons. Preliminary research results on cross-curricular learning communities suggest (although much more research is needed to know if it is true) that more concentrated, longer-term approaches that involve faculty as active, intentional participants will lead to higher retention and greater achievement and development for students (see J. Lucas and Mott 1996; Tinto, Love, and Russo 1994). Further, the research on residence hall learning communities suggests that components related to living and learning—or the equivalent interaction for commuter institutions—should be built into campus learning communities (see Pike, Schroeder, and Berry 1997; Schroeder and Hurst 1996; Schroeder, Mable, and Associates 1994; Winston, Anchors, and Associates 1993). All types of learning communities, however, have been found to bring about significant positive change in students *if they are well done*, so among the factors to consider is what best fits with the institutional culture.

It should be remembered that no matter what models are selected, each professor will also want to make his or her classroom a learning community in and of itself to the extent possible. It should also be remembered that within-class learning communities can work well within any other type of student learning community; instilling collaborative skills and practices is important within any student learning community. Moreover, learning communities need to use technology, such as access to the Internet, for individual and group stimulation, and for communication.

The planned duration of the learning community is an important consideration (J. Lucas and Mott 1996). Although most student learning communities are designed for one semester, additional time together may be desirable to attain more significant long-term impact on students. And if the learning community is effective, participating students will want it to continue after the first semester.

• How do we plan for the development of learning communities?

The best approach is to develop a planning and implementation team comprising selected faculty and student affairs staff that will provide collaborative leadership for the planning, development, and implementation of learning communities. This committee should be chaired by a supportive faculty leader or the vice president or dean of academic affairs with the full support of the president. Program goals and objectives for learning communities within the institutional mission must first be set. Then the focus needs to turn to process strategies and activities for accomplishing development and implementation of the program.

Developing specific objectives for particular learning communities and incorporating those objectives into the institutional mission statement are important (R. Matthews et al. 1997). "These programs seem to succeed when they are incorporated into the curricular mission, not tucked away in the corner of an institution or program. At their best, learning communities are . . . designed to achieve a variety of clearly stated educational goals" (p. 462). Planning and implementation should include an interdisciplinary focus on social and collaborative learning and on the construction of meaning and change, active and experiential student learning, making connections and synthesizing information across knowledge domains and from outside the classroom to the classroom, knowing and considering students' backgrounds and characteristics in setting up student groups, relating values to knowledge within the community, developing a cooperative rather than a competitive environment, and tying multiple courses and semesters or terms into a cohesive package (B. Smith 1993).

The planning committee must decide how best to develop the maximum effectiveness of learning communities, through face-to-face interaction, positive interdependence, individual accountability, or interpersonal, small groups (Johnson, Johnson, and Smith 1991b). Positive interdependence (that is, students in the learning community working together toward a common goal) requires four necessary conditions: (1) face-to-face positive verbal interactions; (2) positive physical interaction when appropriate; (3) maximum contributions by group members; and (4) each member's success contingent upon the success of other group members (Grineski 1996, p. 26). "Specific cognitive processes have been identified as helpful in increasing achievement. [They] include relating new information to what was learned previously, paraphrasing or reviewing information, and checking information" (Slavin 1991a, p. 119).

The team has much to discuss and plan for:

- Students' interests and learning styles and how groups form teams successfully;
- Staffing, consistency, professional development, cooperation, and collaboration of faculty involved in the program;
- How program faculty should work with student learning communities for the maximum impact on students;
- How to ensure the quality of the program;
- How to recruit students to the program;
- How to build members of the group into a team, and how to develop a sense of inclusion, cohesiveness, and group identity;
- How to teach students about self-assessment for the group;
- How to establish expectations for each group of students (they should be high but realistic);
- How to instill in groups a recognition of the competence of low-status students, and how to enhance their social status within the group;
- Which program themes should be emphasized;
- The choice of productive and meaningful open-ended, real-life, significant problems or tasks for the group that demand to know "why," "how," and "how it could have

ended up differently";

- Appropriate team assignments, case studies, and exercises;
- Appropriate exercises that involve "cooperative contro-versy" (Johnson and Johnson 1994b);
- A system to gather feedback and procedures to determine grades for the groups; and
- How the various support services on campus should relate to the groups. A group is only as strong as its weakest link.

The planning team should remember that:

For successful groupwork, students need to learn new and different social skills: how to ask for help and how to assist those who ask for help, how to explain patiently, how to be productive and responsible group members, and how to respect and value other people's contribu-tions. . . . Skills for cooperation and collaboration need to be taught explicitly and practiced consistently before they become internalized, routine behaviors of students in groups. . . . Assigning to students in groups specific pro-cedural roles (e.g., facilitator, materials manager, timer, reporter, recorder, safety officer, harmonizer, and others as necessary) helps the teacher to better delegate author-ity . . . (Shulman, Lotan, and Whitcomb 1995, p. 13).

Students must realize they are responsible for each other's learning as well as their own; thus, the instructor must delegate authority and responsibility to the group. Successful delegation of authority leads to increased discussion and working together as students decide jointly exactly what responsibilities are as-signed to them and how best to deal with the responsibilities. The more they talk and work together, the more they learn.

• What if faculty and staff believe learning commu-nities will take too much time and/or energy?

The learning communities for which research is reported in the previous section were established to conform to standard institutional and departmental operating budgets and work loads (R. Matthews 1994, p. 182). Other learning communi-ties, however, are more intensive, complex, and involved (such as those developed at Drexel University). Moreover, they take significantly more faculty time because professors from different disciplines must carefully integrate course material and spend concentrated, energy-consuming time supporting one another. "The problem is the cost. . . . It involves a lot more faculty time. It's labor intensive. But it gets people talking about common problems of teaching" (Jack C. Kay, chair of the faculty senate at Drexel, cited in Collison 1993, p. A18). After more than half a decade, however, the engineering faculty at Drexel still believe the benefits of their labor-intensive type of learning community—in terms of improved student and faculty outcomes—clearly outweigh the costs. Planning for learning communities must include consideration of such factors as time, energy, and cost.

- **We have many high-risk students. How can learning communities help them?**

The STAR learning community program at Long Beach City College, which focused on high-risk students, found that developing a cohort of students and linking courses through a theme that was important to all those students was very effective (MacKay 1996). The theme in this case was "college success for the basic skills student." (Presumably, a relevant and meaningful theme—and related courses—can be found for any group of students, if one knows group members' interests and the curriculum, and plans carefully.) The STAR project staff also found that the use of workshops, preferably every week, for student learning communities was extremely helpful. Workshops took three different forms: academic skills workshops, informative/reflective workshops, and inspirational, "real-life models" workshops. (The latter two types of workshops should be effective in teaching students in all types of learning communities how to participate effectively in groups.)

High-risk students also needed such special support as supplemental instruction, student work/study subgroups, specialized use of computer labs, and additional noncredit instruction in math. Although cohesive learning communities may be needed for certain types of students with special needs, such as high-risk students, effective use of more diverse student groups—rather than homogeneous groups—is preferable in most cases, as different group members learn differently when they learn together. Good collaboration among students requires group members to have complementary, not the same, skills.

Although cohesive learning communities may be needed for certain types of students with special needs, such as high-risk students, effective use of more diverse student groups—rather than homogeneous groups—is preferable in most cases, as different group members learn differently when they learn together.

- **What is the most common shortcoming related to the optimization of learning communities?**

The most common and critical shortcoming is that the institution is not a bona fide "learning organization" as defined in the first section. If it is not a true learning organization, a college or university tends to be a culture of the traditional (for example, using lectures to teach students) and is afraid of risk. It does not appreciate and reward relevant change. When problems become so apparent they can no longer be ignored, faculty and staff latch onto fads.

Too often the professional development and intellectual involvement of support staff are neglected in institutions that claim to be learning organizations but really are not; a learning organization should encourage and support development in, and involvement by, *all* employees (Kerka 1995; May 1994). "What is different about a learning organization is that it promotes a culture of learning, a community of learners, and it ensures that individual learning enriches and enhances the organization as a whole" (Kerka 1995, p. 3).

Colleges must prepare students to work in business and industry learning organizations (Lyons 1995), which can happen only if the college itself is a true learning organization. The norms of a true learning organization encourage innovation, but innovative organizations may not be learning organizations (Curry 1992). Elaborate structures and chains of command should be eliminated in learning organizations (Gratton 1993); informal learning is important in an organizational learning system (Acebo and Watkins 1988). (See Argyris 1990 for an in-depth discussion of behavioral changes required, and obstacles to overcome, in creating a learning organization.) Clearly, a learning organization requires enlightened executive leadership.

- **What are the basic criteria or guidelines for student learning communities?**

Institutional mission and culture become preeminent in determining whether or not learning communities will be successful. The study group should develop criteria and guidelines, although during start-up, overindulgence in rules and regulations can prevent learning communities from being based on mission and culture. Guidelines are extremely critical to the long-term nature of the project, so their "creators" should use the early parts of this monograph as a foundation for developing institutional guidelines.

• What courses make the best mix for student learning communities?

The faculty on each campus must determine the dynamic mix of courses that will work best for the institution. Large courses coupled with smaller courses often offer the most successful opportunities for facilitating learning communities. Although the research suggests four to six students is the best size for within-class learning communities, no data are available regarding optimum size for other student learning communities. The common optimal size, however, seems to be about 20 to 25 students. It also depends on whether or not a residential component is involved. Those without a residential component need to have some kind of intentional, scheduled activity outside the classroom. Learning teams and learning communities with interaction only in class limit the scope and impact of the team.

• What is an appropriate level of faculty involvement?

Faculty who have classes with institutional learning teams within their sections should be fully aware of the configuration of students. The institution should provide information to faculty about the profile of students in their classrooms and the other classes being taken by the specific learning communities. Thus, faculty of those classes can meet periodically to discuss how they can best relate their course content to other courses to make learning more meaningful across classes. It is even more important that faculty involved in the development of student learning communities become totally aware of the intricate needs of the students and their respective communities. Faculty should receive information about the learning communities as a whole and their specific goals, as well as information related to mentoring students.

• But where are the hard data to support the value of student communities?

A significant number of studies in the higher education literature make it clear that student learning communities result in noteworthy benefits of various kinds for both students and participating faculty. One of the critical elements of success on your campus, however, will be the kind of local data you collect about your learning communities. An assessment team should be created at the very inception of a learning community, and it should include people knowledgeable about the design of studies, the reliability and validity of measures and indicators, and effective data collection. These studies should be longitudinal and should include information about students' persistence, achievement, and satisfaction; levels of faculty and student interaction; other learning outcomes; and the college environment. Although such studies may be burdensome to faculty (even when they are given credit toward promotion and tenure for their involvement in such pedagogical research) and to students, it is the only way to prepare for the longevity of learning communities. If we are not diligent in this area, learning communities will become a fad that recycles every 30 or 40 years.

• **How should we publicize our learning communities?**
Beloit College, the Universities of Michigan, Missouri, and Maryland, and others have prepared attractive brochures to recruit students for participation in learning communities. If your institution plans to develop such promotional materials, it should be done as a quality job. Encourage student participants to tell prospective students about how learning communities have benefited them. Highlight the communities in press releases about participating students sent to hometown newspapers, in stories in alumni bulletins and newspapers, and on television and radio, and on the institution's Web page. A major contributor to the success of learning communities is public relations and marketing. It is up to the institution to sell the idea to the appropriate publics.

• **What are the keys for maximizing the impact of residential learning communities, and what impact will such groups have on the residence hall system?**
Residential life educators should work closely with faculty to create student learning communities around "common educational aspirations" (Schroeder 1993, p. 521); it is important to integrate inside- and outside-class experiences for students. Efforts should especially be made to enhance students' first-year experience, because institutional bonding is an important factor in retention. Schroeder's models for creating authentic communities based on involvement, investment, influence,

and identity are also applicable to a broader interpretation of learning communities. Clearly, they could serve as principles for the creation of effective learning communities.

Faculty and academic administrators interested in creating residential life communities would do well to read *Student Housing and Residential Life* (Winston, Anchors, and Associates 1993), particularly the chapters on developing and enhancing student communities, program design, and developmental impacts of campus living environments (see also Winston, Bonney, Miller, and Dagley 1988). If a learning community involves a living-learning component, it will likely have an impact on the current learning environment within the residence hall—positive or negative—depending on the local situation. Many residence systems have organized living units. The infusion of a different organizational structure may disrupt the current system, which will require a major effort by residence hall staff to ensure students' acceptance.

Concluding Remarks
"Service learning is the ultimate learning community" (Cross 1998, p. 10). If well done, such activity fits with the following six principles for effective student learning communities:

1. *Learning communities are generally small, unique, and cohesive units characterized by a common sense of purpose and powerful peer influences.*
2. *Student interaction within learning communities should be characterized by the four I's—involvement, investment, influence, and identity.*
3. *Learning communities involve bounded territory that provides easy access to and control of group space that supports ongoing interaction and social stability.*
4. *Learning communities should be primarily student centered, not staff centered, if they are to promote student learning. Staff must assume that students are capable and responsible young adults who are primarily responsible for the quality and extent of their learning.*
5. *Effective learning communities should be the result of collaborative partnerships between faculty, students, and residence hall staff. Learning communities should not be created in a vacuum; they are designed to intentionally achieve specific educational outcomes.*
6. *Finally, learning communities should exhibit a clear set*

of values and normative expectations for active partici-
pation. The normative peer cultures of learning commu-
nities enhance student learning and development in
specific ways (Schroeder 1994, p. 183).

Despite the complexities, intentional and well-planned and
-implemented student learning communities will have much
more positive impact than anticipated if colleges become
fully committed to effective learning communities and if they
do them well. All of a college's learners—students, faculty,
and staff—must be engaged in such a community.

LEARNING COMMUNITIES IN THE FUTURE

*The efficacy of technology itself is not in question; . . .
studies have consistently demonstrated that the achievement and satisfaction of students who learn via technology can equal those of students in regular classrooms.
Instead, the focus is on surrounding issues, such as
[whether] students in "virtual" learning situations [will]
be isolated, with no semblance of human contact with
their instructors* (Johnstone and Krauth 1996, p. 39).

The focus of this section is on future developments and directions related to learning communities. Much has been accomplished in the area of physical interaction in student learning
communities and a large literature base pertains to the subject,
but much more development and refinement remain. Learning
organizations as learning communities have only recently re-
ceived much attention related to their application in education, and proactive faculty learning communities have yet to
receive real attention on most campuses. This section discusses the current status of, and developments and projections
within, each primary membership category of learning communities, and then turns to the rapidly evolving concept and
potential reality of "virtual learning communities." (Because no
studies could be found that deal with "correspondent learning
communities" and that area seems relatively unimportant compared with the other categories, that concept and its development are not included in this discussion.)

Student Learning Communities

A nationwide reform movement in higher education, student
learning communities began in the early 1990s. Although the
movement has far to go (R. Matthews et al. 1997), student
learning communities clearly have dramatic power to revital-
ize the effectiveness of education at all levels in this country.

Preliminary evidence suggests that some student learning
communities have more positive impact than others, but the
evidence is not clear-cut and the studies were not designed
specifically for such comparison. Thus, the most important
documented factor in their success is how effectively the
learning communities are being implemented in terms of students' productive involvement and within-group collaboration
and cooperation. Until definitive evidence exists that some
types of student learning communities are superior to others,
the type of student learning community to be used, when all

are well done, depends on such factors as what seems most relevant and appropriate for a particular group of students.

It is unclear from the available data what faculty-produced preparatory exercises, faculty styles, and faculty/staff action plans—for different settings and types of students—will maximize students' participation in learning communities and their potential to learn, persist, and be satisfied, despite a report that "the practice of putting students in groups without a notion of the relevance of the groups for learning . . . has given way to greater understanding about when groups are appropriate and not appropriate, how to construct them, and how to design effective exercises and problems" (Gamson 1994, p. 46).

Determining which student learning communities and combinations thereof are most effective must be a primary focus in the future. Equally important is determining how to optimize the performance and effectiveness of student learning communities of different kinds. Research is also needed on how to motivate faculty to participate fully in student learning communities, on the characteristics of students who do not participate, and on how to motivate them.

In late 1996, a project funded by the Fund for the Improvement of Postsecondary Education was announced whose purpose is to "create a network of 20 'adopting institutions' working to more fully establish their curricular learning community programs.

In late 1996, a project funded by the Fund for the Improvement of Postsecondary Education was announced whose purpose is to "create a network of 20 'adopting institutions' working to more fully establish their curricular learning community programs, and to extend their experience and knowledge to a larger national audience through a major national learning communities conference in 1999. . . . [It] will work collaboratively to strengthen their programs, share best practices, address problems, and assess [results]" (Washington Center 1996, p. 1). This effort will be a helpful resource for assistance in making learning communities as effective as possible. Moreover, new tools of technology, such as high-powered personal computers, multimedia, and inquiry-based instruction, are available to assist in developing learning communities (Kerns 1996). In the future, we will need to know how such technology can best facilitate the establishment and effectiveness of communities.

Learning Organizations
The stimulation for business and industry, and colleges and universities (or a subunit, such as a university library [Phipps 1993]) to become "learning organizations" arose from the writings of Peter Senge (1990, 1994a, 1994b). Other authors

in higher education, such as Ernest Boyer, however, led the way for colleges and universities to become "learning organizations" before Senge became prominent.

The development of learning organizations in higher education

Only recently has the higher education literature devoted much attention to colleges' and universities' becoming learning organizations. Few colleges and universities have yet become true learning organizations, but it must happen if student learning communities are to become their most effective. The situation should improve markedly if college administrators and others in higher education direct attention toward learning organizations and extensive research into them.

Ernest Boyer's vision was to have the new American college "connect the disconnects" and "make the college years a more holistic, fulfilling experience for students" (cited in Coye 1997, p. 21). Boyer's "scholarship of engagement" is the epitome of a learning community. His message speaks of learning communities and what they mean to faculty and students engaged in inquiry for meaning in life. Boyer was clearly a visionary. His ideals of the integration of campus life, service, and scholarship focused on the quality of community in enhancing the educational enterprise.

If education is to exercise a moral force in society, the process must take place in a moral context. It must occur in communities that are held together not by pressure or coercion, not by accident of history, but by shared purposes and goals, by simple acts of kindness, and by the respect group members have for one another. . . . This tradition and conviction will be maintained only [if] there is a continuing commitment to community here today (Ernest Boyer, cited in Coye 1997, p. 26).

The "new American college" has three priorities: (1) to clarify the curriculum, (2) to connect the world beyond the classroom, and (3) to create a campus community (Coye 1997). The third priority, involving the most implications for developing powerful learning communities, calls for a return to "community and the moral character of students" (p. 25).

The principles for a campus community listed in the first section (see pp. 6–7) must serve as the foundation for learning organizations in higher education. They are extremely important, given their application throughout the academic community: "They apply to students, faculty, and administration; to academic work, services in the outside community, and the day-to-day living on the campus" (Coye 1997, p. 25).

Senge's five learning disciplines (1994b), which he refers to as a "body of techniques" (p. 7) to enhance the development of a learning community, provide the core knowledge for establishing a learning organization and ultimately a foundation for all "learning communities." His five "disciplines"—personal mastery, mental models, shared vision, team learning, and systems thinking—are key ingredients to the sustenance for creating learning communities. Thoughtful integration of these five disciplines is the key to enhancing the success of learning organizations. Fundamental to the practice is to provide all members of the organization (the community) with the incentive and the desire to take control of their own learning through *personal mastery*. No learning community will ever be successful without empowering learners through a variety of techniques.

Mental models are "the images, assumptions, and stories [that] we carry in our minds of ourselves, other people, institutions, and every aspect of the world" (Senge 1994b, p. 235). They become crucial in that an individual's insight and picture of the importance of the learning community determine in part the quality of the learning community itself. Mental models shape individuals' actions and thoughts about the world around them.

Shared vision is the creation of an understanding of the possibilities. The connectedness of learners in the classroom, the creation of environments and synergy toward empowerment beyond the boundaries of traditional learning paradigms, and the sense of worth from sharing and engaging in learning are powerful indicators of and preparation for lifelong learning.

Team learning moves learning from an individual activity to a shared activity involving several people. Breaking down previously held beliefs about individual learning and individual performance is a key to developing the powerful environment of a successful learning community. We must begin to teach the concept of team in our laboratories and classrooms.

At the crux of all these disciplines is ultimately *systems thinking*. If we are to incorporate the value of learning communities beyond the classroom, we must begin to think about how we make these learning communities an integral part of the institutional system.

The challenge for all learning organizations is to provide some format, forum, or avenue for preparation in dealing with the world's larger social and economic issues. Senge's concept of the learning organization is a powerful undergirding structure for broadening our understanding of learning communities to create such a forum. The integration of Senge's concepts—along with the thoughts of Dewey, Meiklejohn, and the innovators on our campuses today—provides a marriage that will harness the potential of how people will learn and work together to lead productive, successful, and challenging lives. The integration of these concepts can also lead to powerful stimulation and support for change (J.S. Brown 1997).

Reorganizing and refocusing learning should become the centerpiece of the higher education enterprise (Wingspread Group 1993). This reorganized and refocused learning, along with the focus on learning organizations in business, has provided impetus for the development of learning organizations in higher education. Further, "for the remaining few years of this century, 'The Learning Revolution' will . . . be a leading theme of articles, books, conferences, commissions, studies, and hopefully practica in education" (O'Banion 1997, p. 1). Higher education has and will be fundamentally changed by this revolution.

What is being talked about is a totally new paradigm for collegiate undergraduate education—a shift from teaching to learning (R. Barr and Tagg 1995). "One outcome of the paradigm shift will be transformation of our colleges and universities, from the 'teaching factories' or 'educational shopping malls' they too often resemble, into authentic 'learning communities'" (Angelo 1997, p. 3). The "seven positive shifts" in operating procedures include:

- A culture of inquiry and evidence;
- A culture of explicit, broadly shared goals, criteria, and standards;
- A teaching culture that applies relevant knowledge to improve practices;
- A broader, more inclusive vision of scholarship;
- An academic culture that attempts to realistically account for costs;

- A culture that encourages collaboration for the common good *and* individual advancement; and
- A model of higher education that is qualitative and transformative (Angelo 1997).

Angelo's *shifts* can be employed "to construct a more productive, learning-focused campus" when combined in a meaningful manner with his "seven proven *levers*":

- Assessment;
- The faculty evaluation system;
- New models and methods of accounting;
- Methods to set goals, criteria, and standards;
- Literature on research and practice in teaching and learning;
- Cooperative and collaborative methods of education;
- Competency-based, mastery learning (Angelo 1997).

St. Gregory's College (now St. Gregory's University) illustrates the potential of learning organizations in practice. At a conference in Oklahoma City in December 1996, two administrators from this Benedictine college in Oklahoma told Oscar Lenning that enrollment in the college had decreased over a number of years until the institution's very survival seemed threatened. After the arrival of an empowering president, however, enrollment increased 40 percent in each of the next two years.

Bacone College, where Lenning had arrived as a consultant less than a year earlier, had similarly experienced several years of declining enrollment and severe financial straits, resulting in depression and low morale in the college community. Arrangements were made for all senior administrators at Bacone, plus faculty and staff who expressed an interest, to visit St. Gregory's College and observe for themselves that a major improvement in college enrollments is possible, even in very severe cases of previously declining enrollments.

At the beginning of the visit, St. Gregory's College President Frank Pfaff spoke to the group and suggested that a number of institutionwide, specific changes had led to the turnaround in enrollments. The two most important factors were that the college had become a real, institutionwide learning organization, and that it had reviewed and renewed its commitment to the college's Benedictine roots. Pfaff then distributed copies of an article titled "Universities as Learning

Organizations" (Tinto 1997b), St. Gregory's case document for a five-year fundraising campaign, *The Renaissance Plan: A Comprehensive Plan for the Renewal of St. Gregory's College,* a theological article titled "Change," and the Winter 1997 issue of the college's magazine for alumni and friends that contained an article titled "The Era of Transformation" (Pfaff 1997). Other speakers, including faculty and staff, emphasized how the college had become a true learning organization and gave concrete examples of how this concept had become real and exciting throughout the entire campus community.

The within-class tribes learning communities described earlier cannot be effective until the total school becomes a "tribes school"—or "a learning community where teachers, administrators, students, and parents enjoy the mutual respect and caring essential for growth and development" (Gibbs 1994, p. 24).

> *Building learning organizations . . . requires basic shifts in how we think and interact. The changes go beyond individual corporate cultures, or even the culture of Western management; they penetrate to the bedrock assumptions and habits of our culture as a whole. We are discovering that moving forward is an exercise in personal commitment and community building. As Dr. W. Edwards Deming says, nothing happens without "personal transformation." And the only safe space to allow this transformation is a learning community. . . . We are coming to see our efforts as building "communities of commitment." Without commitment, the hard work required will never be done* (Kofman and Senge 1993, p. 5).

This shift is comparable to the revolutionary shift in thinking that Galileo brought to his world (Kofman and Senge 1993).

The importance for student learning communities of the institution's becoming a learning organization

The first section of this monograph emphasizes the importance of coming together and of a commitment to "celebrating, mourning, and risking together" (Sullivan 1994).

> *Creating learning communities, we are discovering, requires fundamental shifts in how we think, interact, and view the world around us. . . . As we move from viewing fragmented pieces to seeing the whole, from self*

*to community, from problem solving to creating, and
from absolute truths to coherent interpretations, the
potential for creating and sustaining learning communities increases. In a learning community, we begin to
commit to a vision for creating a world of increasing
interdependency and change. It is not what the vision
is but what the vision does that matters. . . . These kinds
of relationships . . . increase our capacity for learning
collaboratively* (Sullivan 1994, p. 14).

Creating effective student learning communities requires
changes in how we think and perceive, and how colleges
are organized. Institutions should make three organizational
changes:

*First, colleges and universities would adopt a community
model of academic organization that would promote
involvement through the use of shared, connected learning experiences among its members, students and faculty
alike. Second, colleges and universities, four-year ones in
particular, would reorganize the first year of college as a
distinct unit in its own underlying logic and pedagogical
orientation. Third, colleges and universities would reorganize faculty workload to allow them, as well as their
students, to cross the disciplinary and departmental
borders that now divide them* (Tinto 1998, p. 170).

Creating learning communities requires us to thoroughly
understand the interactions and relationships among leadership, shared community vision, the building of community,
cooperative/collaborative learning, systems approaches, and
models of thinking and personal mastery (Kofman and Senge
1993). As noted, "the only safe space to allow [personal]
transformation is a learning community" (W.E. Deming, cited
in Kofman and Senge 1993, p. 5). Thus, for truly effective
student learning communities to occur, the institution needs
to become a learning organization. Moreover, some of the
operational concepts found effective for learning organizations also pertain to student learning communities.

Applying Senge's disciplines
Senge (1990) indicated that "learning communities" learn to
continuously innovate by applying the five disciplines, which

are never fully mastered . Although all the disciplines are important for an effective learning community, systems thinking, the fifth discipline, is central. And dialogue among all group members is the key to it (Isaacs 1994). Effective dialogue maximizes group learning, knowledge, and understanding. "The capacity for great conversations about things that matter is essential for breakthrough thinking and collaborative innovation" (Senge, Kleiner, Roberts, Ross, and Smith 1994, p. 526).

Perhaps the best way for a college or university to become a true learning organization as envisioned by Senge would be to apply the operating principles of continuous quality improvement (CQI) and total quality management (TQM) (Freed, Klugman, and Fife 1997). A conceptual framework, developed by Fife, would include:

> *(1) Vision, mission, and outcomes driven: What is your aim? (2) Systems dependent: How do the parts fit together? (3) Leadership: Who leads the creation of a new culture? (4) Decisions based on fact: How do you update your knowledge? (5) Delegation of decision making: How do you make decisions? (6) Collaboration: Who makes the decisions? (7) Systematic individual development: How do you improve? (8) Planning for change: How do you prepare for the future? (9) Leadership: How are the changes supported?* (Freed and Klugman 1996, p. 2).

The quality principles seem to reflect Senge's learning organization disciplines.

During a study cosponsored by the ERIC Clearinghouse on Higher Education and The George Washington University, Freed and Klugman conducted site interviews at 10 colleges and universities known to be active in implementing CQI/TQM for at least 10 years (1996). Their findings make clear that a college can become a true learning organization by using CQI/TQM (see also Cleveland and Plastrik 1995; Finaly-Neumann and Neumann 1995; Hubbard and Gilmour 1996; Loehr 1994).

Operating principles for building community (J.B. Brown, Smith, and Isaacs 1994) help bring people together into a rich learning environment and develop learning communities:

- Focus on real work (quality learning and instruction);
- Keep it simple;

- Act (learn by doing);
- See the glass as half full, not as half empty;
- Seek what unifies;
- Do it when people are ready;
- Design (and facilitate) space where community can happen;
- Find and cultivate the informal leader;
- Learn to host good gatherings (classes);
- Acknowledge people's contributions;
- Involve the whole person;
- Celebrate.

Certain "core processes" are essential for creating and sustaining learning organizations and other learning communities (Senge et al. 1994). The members of learning organizations (as well as other types of learning communities) mutually encourage learning and improvement among the others, and are mutually committed to continuing and sustaining the learning community. All members are aware of how important their contributions are to the learning community as a whole. In addition, members perpetuate the memory of its history and traditions by sharing relevant stories with all new members, and they collaborate effectively in developing consistent and ongoing interdependence.

These characteristics of an effective learning organization must also be true of student and faculty learning communities. They are essential if students are to say, "I'm glad I experienced a learning community." To optimize the effectiveness of student learning communities, we must determine effective ways not only to bring them together, but also to promote group members' commitment to celebrating together, mourning together, and risking together.

Faculty Learning Communities
As originally conceived, faculty disciplinary associations are akin to what we have called "learning communities." Learning communities in this category may include students, but faculty are the predominant participants and leaders. Discipline-based communities may also include scholars from outside education, (see, e.g., Choi 1995). Some professional societies have study groups that some people have called "action communities." For professional and disciplinary associations in general, we would argue for more intentional subcommunities that focus on improving students' learning, such as those

formed within the American Association for Higher Education. Professional and disciplinary associations should become more intentional, effective learning communities in the future. Too often, such associations—and faculty colleagues—pay lip service to the idea of learning communities but do not engage in true, bona fide, effective learning communities.

Institutions of higher education were originally intended to be faculty learning communities (see Brubacher and Rudy 1976) and ideally still should be, but the pressures of organizational structures and reward systems have created "stand-alone fiefdoms" that have limited real innovation (Blau 1994). The majority of the literature about faculty in learning communities is found in the literature about student learning communities. Virtually no literature discusses the specific topic of faculty learning communities, and the reason is the prevailing view that faculty work involves conducting and being evaluated for their teaching, research/scholarship/writing, and community service. Some commentators discuss faculty work as discipline-based or institution-based (Blau 1994; Fairweather 1996), while others describe it as discipline-, profession-, and/or institution-based (Dunn, Rouse, and Seff 1994).

When asked to identify their learning community, faculty generally indicate their discipline or their institution, depending on the mission of the institution that employs them. Faculty at research universities tend to be more discipline-based (and their learning communities international), while those at small liberal arts colleges and community colleges tend to be institution-based. Often, the professional reward structure (focused on individual production), the number of faculty in the department, and institutional resources, in great measure, determine faculty members' identity with a learning community.

The development of learning communities at community colleges and liberal arts colleges, however, is usually associated with the institution's instructional mission. These colleges seem to have created the majority of strong learning communities based on the concept that teaching is important. For them, faculty learning communities are an extension of teaching.

Fairweather's categories of faculty behavior include *instruction* and *research:*

1. Instruction *is not limited to classroom teaching. It includes time spent working with student organizations; formal classroom instruction; independent instruction;*

Institutions of higher education were originally intended to be faculty learning communities (see Brubacher and Rudy 1976) and ideally still should be, but the pressures of organizational structures and reward systems have created "stand-alone fiefdoms" that have limited real innovation.

noncredit instruction; advising, counseling, and super-
vising students; and grading papers, preparing courses,
and developing new curricula.

2. Research *includes measures of time spent on research*
and scholarship, including preparing for and conduct-
ing research, preparing or reviewing articles or books,
attending professional meetings, giving performances in
the fine or applied arts, and seeking outside funding for
research (1996, p. 24).

Junior faculty are usually encouraged (almost required) to
shun involvement in learning communities (as defined by this
report) if they wish to be promoted and receive tenure (Fairweather 1996). Moreover, most of the experimental and cluster
colleges (early learning communities) failed because of conflicts
among the faculty regarding the disciplines and undergraduate
education (Fairweather 1996). One of the most identifiable results was that faculty involved in those early learning communities did not earn tenure because of the institution's requirement
to publish or perish. It is doubtful that faculty work will change
markedly unless the reward structure and support for undergraduate education (and learning communities) become institutionalized into, and rewarded by, the process involved in promoting faculty and granting tenure. And they must be
institutionalized to the point of making a difference.

As shown in the case study discussed in "Creating and
Implementing Optimal College Student Learning Communities," true faculty learning communities focusing on improving pedagogy can work even in research universities.

Virtual Learning Communities
"Virtual learning communities" make up one category of
what is referred to in the first section of this monograph as
the "primary form of interaction" dimension of learning communities. Although this discussion could be directly linked
with student learning communities, it also pertains to faculty
learning communities and learning organizations.

Faculty in general are slow to adopt the new technologies:

Academic pundits frequently comment that the pace of
innovation in higher education can be measured by
the 40 years it took to get the overhead projector out of
the bowling alley into the classroom. The [few] pundits

who know something about both bowling and technol-
ogy often add that faculty are now far more likely to
find computerized projection screens in bowling alleys
than in college classrooms (Green 1996, p. 24).

But information technology "has finally emerged as a perma-
nent, respected, and increasingly essential component of the
college experience" (p. 24).

The use of electronic mail, in one instance, created a true
sense of community in a graduate reading class (Anderson and
Lee 1995). The on-line communication among class members
provided mutual support and led to the sharing of ideas and
information, risk taking by individuals and groups, reflection
on learning by individuals and groups, and cooperative learning. Computers can contribute to collaborative and cooperative learning (see Crook 1994; Davies 1988; McConnell 1994).

With most faculty and students linked to the Internet, the
stage is set for the formation of a multitude of virtual learning communities among students, faculty, and others. The
question now becomes one of how learning in virtual learning communities can be promoted and maximized.

Some fundamentals of virtual learning communities
Computer networks are based on the same concepts as communities. Moreover, educational networks on the Internet
have been proliferating (Clement and Abrahams 1994), most
colleges have local-area networks (LANs), and many colleges
and universities are heavily involved in distance education. A
1995 study by the U.S. Department of Education* found that
one-third of all colleges and universities offered distance
education courses, with another quarter planning to do so in
the next three years. The University of Maryland, for example, had 5,700 distance education college graduates in 1997
(R. Lucas 1998).

Presumably, most of the categories and subcategories of
student learning communities discussed in the second section of this monograph could be formed and conducted on-
line. One regularly hears about close personal relationships
that result solely from communicating with others through
Internet chat rooms, even though no eye contact occurs and

---

*The study, NCES No. 98303, was released in February 1998 as a data set on
CD-ROM and diskette. See the NCES Web site, *http://www.nces.ed.gov/*.

body language cannot be observed. Any chat group that is formed for the purposes of its members' sharing their learning with others and for learning together as a group is, in effect, a virtual learning community. The variety of virtual learning communities possible is limitless.

Student learning in virtual communities is expanding rapidly. Six institutions (including Web addresses) with Web-based models extend "student learning . . . and student affairs programming into [students'] homes" (Seabreeze 1997, p. 102). An instructional systems design (ISD) model for creating on-line "learning communities" emphasizes both cooperative and collaborative learning (Ravitz 1997), but users should note that "when poorly implemented, the redefinition and blurring of roles can lead to chaos and confusion" (p. 10).

Treuer and Belote (1997) identify current and emerging applications that can promote students' involvement and learning through virtual student learning communities, and then provide a glimpse of the future through a vignette about a student's academic career. Learning can start with exploring the options for college when a student is still in high school. It can continue through graduation, through virtual learning communities that are part of a student's classroom experiences, such as a first-year course labeled Introduction to College Learning, and residential life. And it can continue through career planning and placement into the workplace as the student establishes and develops a virtual meeting room for the job. Students are connected through a worldwide virtual community.

Two principles are important in the development of virtual learning communities: (1) Make certain the learning communities are student-centered and focused on a common goal, and (2) make certain that components on preparation, planning, and reflection are included in the plans for learning communities (Treuer and Belote 1997). A number of "principles of good practice for electronically offered academic degree and certificate programs" pertain to curriculum and instruction, institutional context and commitment to role and mission, faculty support, resources for learning, students and student services, commitment to support, and evaluation/assessment (Johnstone and Krauth 1996, p. 40). A primary concern in such programs is the amount and quality of, and the resources available to support, interaction between students and faculty and among students.

In the computer age, the nature of knowledge is changing from static to fluid (Wolfson 1995, pp. 24–29). Thus, we must rethink the purposes of education and the definition of what is truth. In this new era, traditional classroom instruction will no longer be appropriate, and professors with their students must become "seekers of knowledge" in a learning community. As distance learning becomes prominent, instructors and their students may never meet in person, as learning communities of the future are likely to become global through the Internet and the World Wide Web (Wolfson 1995).

A definitive study of the virtual classroom environment, although a study of graduate students involving only one five-week summer course, may have relevance and meaning for undergraduate student virtual learning communities, particularly those focusing on older, employed students (Powers and Mitchell 1997). The graduate course was offered entirely over the Internet, using electronic mail, listserv, chat rooms, Web pages, and so on. During synchronous chat room sessions, the instructor was definitely the "head of the class," and during asynchronous (listserv) communication, the instructor was a learner in the learning community as much as the students. The data collected included e-mail messages, listserv data records, transcripts of chat sessions, and an on-site end-of-course group interview that was videotaped for later analysis. The Internet does indeed lend itself to recording archival data.

The authors found four factors to be significantly related to students' performance and reported perceptions of electronic learning communities: (1) students' support of each other; (2) interaction among students; (3) interaction between students and faculty; and (4) time demands of the course.

Based on the amount of rapport that developed among students, the amount of support students gave to one another, the quality of interactions among students and the relationships that developed, and the amount and quality of students' learning engendered by the virtual learning community, Powers and Mitchell concluded that the virtual classroom in this study had become a genuine learning community, despite the large distances separating everyone throughout the course, and despite students and instructors not having face-to-face contact. The authors concluded it is possible to develop and maintain positive student-student and student-faculty interactions in a virtual classroom that may not be possible in a regular classroom (as students feel freer to share personal matters). The results also suggest that the asynchronous tools can also be used to enrich dialogue and discussion in a class that meets in person.

Instructional software designed for individual rather than group use poses a special challenge for virtual learning communities (Sullivan 1994). Software packages designed to develop, facilitate, and enhance collaborative learning within learning communities are needed.

Certain generalizations about virtual learning communities apply to the development and implementation of all student learning communities (Dudgeon 1995). Learning communities should be organized around specific themes or intellectual tasks, but before faculty can create effective learning communities, they must have themselves participated in such a learning community. Faculty learning communities should be formed to train faculty in their new roles in creating and sustaining student learning communities. Faculty need to change their focus from traditional teaching to the teacher serving as facilitator, manager, and coach of the "interactive environment" (Hannafin and Savenye 1993), and an ideal vision about their future role (Kouzes and Posner 1987) must be a driving force.

Moreover, the college or university should undertake a pilot project for the creation of a learning community, applying a "humanness model" (Lippitt 1981) for bringing about change, before beginning implementation of learning communities on a broad scale. Faculty meeting together as a faculty learning community can explore instructors' responsibilities, students' responsibilities, and instructional models from the literature, among other topics, "in an environment of trust, sharing, and collaboration [that will] empower teachers by giving them the technological tools for their new teacher roles, while building relationships with mentors and sponsors" (Dudgeon 1995, pp. 7–8). Faculty should be charged with the development of a plan for creating and sustaining student learning communities, and they should celebrate all the small successes they experience as a group throughout the process to keep up their energy and momentum. Participants should become mentors for other faculty. A key to success is developing a belief among all participants that student learning communities are important for maximum learning to occur and that "a climate of trust, collaboration, sharing, and caring is essential to enable people to learn and grow" (p. 10).

Other authors agree that the same factors important in establishing and maintaining effective site-based communities are important for establishing and maintaining on-line virtual learning communities (Groff 1996). E-mail is an important factor that gives students the opportunity to interact with and ask questions of faculty, whether the venue is a virtual community or a site-based learning community (Freud 1996).

Virtual learning communities of the future

Cooperation among colleges and universities through the use of the Internet and computer technology such as videoconferencing—that is not limited by proximity of location—could create virtual learning communities that can lead to improved enrollment figures and expanded services to on-campus students at participating institutions. Significant improvements in educational quality and economies of scale could be achieved through such cooperation, especially at diverse small colleges that emphasize personal attention and values as their special strengths.

Using the Internet and videoconferencing software and equipment could help create "virtual academic departments." One- and two-person academic departments at small colleges leave faculty isolated in terms of day-to-day collegial interaction, especially with regard to discipline-based program planning and evaluation. In addition, students have extremely limited direct exposure to, and one-on-one interaction with, faculty in their major. This problem can be overcome if academic departments at small colleges with disparate locations join together to form virtual academic departments comprising faculty from different schools of thought within the discipline.

All faculty in a virtual department would be involved through the Internet in several ways:

- Decisions about the creation of cooperative courses to be shared through the Internet;
- Cooperative research of resources on the Internet and elsewhere for such courses;
- The establishment of policies and procedures for the virtual department;

Using the Internet and videoconferencing software and equipment could help create "virtual academic departments."

- Ongoing advice and interaction with students of the virtual department, one on one or in groups;
- Scheduled departmental meetings;
- A mentor of chat sessions with all students majoring in the discipline at the participating institutions;
- Cooperative faculty professional development, consultation, and support over the Internet; and
- Program planning, evaluation, and review for the virtual department.

Current courses and programs at each of the colleges that are unavailable at the other participating colleges would suddenly become available to students at all participating schools. Some of these courses and programs could be modified into attractive new versions to generate additional revenue for all participants. Each participating college undoubtedly knows distinctive courses and programs it would like to offer, but insufficient demand from students makes it infeasible to justify offering them. Participating colleges could jointly create a cooperative version of such courses and programs that would be made available to students at all participating institutions, as well as offered through the Internet to other students.

All institutions participating in the virtual departments would receive significant benefits with regard to the recruitment of students, even if they were competing for many of the same students. Cooperative promotion, in addition to individual promotion, would lead to increased student enrollments at all the participating institutions. Courses offered by a virtual department could even be made available to others in their homes or offices.

A virtual education community could also look like the one suggested by Bertrand (1994). Communication of subject matter between professor and learner tends not to be effective because the student culture is so disparate from faculty and college institutional cultures. Thus, a generic common culture needs to be created so the exchange of information will not be hindered. A priority should be placed on creating an educational communication system based on a common culture, or a "virtual educational community" (Bertrand 1994). Although not what he had in mind, perhaps the only hope for such a virtual community is through the Internet.

Increasingly, the international focus is on virtual universities that emphasize distance learning, the latest in technology and curriculum, and older students. There were a total of 11 virtual universities in spring 1997, each serving more than 100,000 students (Daniel 1997). Those virtual universities, none of which are located in the United States, served a total group of 2.8 million students worldwide. The average annual expenditure per student for these virtual universities in 1997–98 was $350—compared with $12,500 per student for all U.S. colleges and universities (p. 14). With labor costs and other economic factors considered, however, the cost differential between virtual and traditional universities was more on the order of one to ten. The British Open University, the largest and most prominent virtual university in the world, ranks in the top 20 of all British universities in terms of learning quality and results (p. 13).

Western Governors University (WGU), the first U.S. virtual university, had its Smart Catalog on line in 1998. (Midwestern and middle Atlantic states, and several foreign countries, are considering participation in WGU.) Initially offering two associate degree programs, WGU is also serving as a clearinghouse for on-line courses being offered by colleges and universities in the 18 participating states. Although it is not yet clear what form WGU eventually will take, it is clear that learning communities will focus on competencies for learners (it will not offer credit for courses taken), cut across many state lines, and draw its courses from a large variety of institutions.* The officially approved principles of good practice for electronically offered degree and certificate programs were designed to guide WGU's development and implementation (Johnstone and Krauth 1996). These principles emphasize overcoming the isolation of students and incorporating student-faculty interaction as primary problems to address.†

Rather than be a part of WGU, California chose to form its own California Virtual University,** which is not a true virtual university because it will not offer degrees; it will serve only as an on-line clearinghouse for courses offered on the Internet by California colleges and universities. The Southern Re-

---

*For the latest information about WGU, contact *http://www.wgu.edu.*
†Since this report was written in summer 1998, it was announced in fall 1998 that WGU and the British Open University would merge.
***http://www.virtualu.ca.gov/.*

gional Education Board piloted its 15-state Southern Regional Electronic Campus* in spring 1998 and expected to list over 1,000 courses by fall 1998. Arizona Learning Systems, a cooperative effort of Arizona rural and urban community colleges, will "create a virtual branch campus of every community college district" in the state (Dailey and Hassler 1997, p. 57).

"Virtual campuses" and "virtual classrooms" (Twigg and Oblinger 1997) are being implemented by colleges and universities in almost every state. In Oklahoma, for example, institutions are participating in both WGU and the Southern Regional Electronic Campus, and will participate in the electronic campus being developed by the Oklahoma State Regents for Higher Education. Oklahoma community colleges will also participate in the Electronic Community College of Oklahoma, which is in the early stages of development.

A comparison of virtual and traditional university educational processes notes that:

> *Your instructional system is driven by teaching rather than by learning; by the needs of professors rather than students. . . . The teacher communicates with students in a network of classrooms in real time; it is a teacher-centered form of education. . . . Under the individual learning scenario, you've created the classroom in thousands of homes, so it has to be a student-centered approach. You must figure out what constitutes an effective home learning environment for the student* (Daniel 1997, pp. 14–15).

Virtual universities use technology of various kinds to assist instructors to be more caring and effective in assisting students to learn, with "learning communities" being the key to educational success:

> *Virtual universities have a . . . commitment to providing a "seamless educational continuum" for lifelong learners in a collaborative, caring environment. . . . The key to accomplishing the new vision of excellence and quality in meeting the needs of adult learners through alternative computer-based curriculum deliv-*

---

*http://www.srec.sreb.org/.

ery methodologies will be in creating and sustaining learning communities (Dudgeon 1995, pp. 5–6).

In Iowa, the Iowa Communications Network has served as the basis for sharing courses among colleges and allowing high school students to take college-level courses at their local school via a full-resolution, audiovisual fiber-optic network. Kirkwood Community College, Iowa Central Community College, and others have extensive distance education offerings available on the Web that have student learning communities as one of their core values. Moreover, Kirkwood has taken the lead in joining with seven other leading distance learning community colleges across the nation (in Arizona, California, Florida, Ohio, and Texas) to form the Community College Distance Learning Network (Blumenstyk 1998), which jointly advertised, in *USA Today,* big-city newspapers, and featured spots on Yahoo! and other Internet sites, the availability of 500 courses through the Internet in fall 1998.

Students and professors in a virtual learning community may never meet in person, because such a learning community may have members across a wide geographical area. Indeed, virtual learning communities may have global participants. Scientists in particular fields, for example, might participate in worldwide networks, sharing newly discovered information and conducting ongoing discussions with one another over the Internet.

The emergence of Internet II should be monitored for possible implications for virtual student learning communities. Along with new technologies and innovations related to compressed video and satellite transmission, these innovations have major implications for creating distinctive kinds of learning communities. Principles and procedures for creating and sustaining virtual learning communities are not only emerging, but also being refined. (See Groff 1996 for an in-depth conceptual discussion of establishing and sustaining on-line communities and their implications for higher education, and Freud 1996 for a description of the implications of the virtual community for community colleges.)

Concluding Remarks

Too often mere lip service is paid to the concept of community in higher education—whether one is dealing with learning organizations, faculty learning communities, or student learning communities—which means the powerful potential of this concept goes unrealized. The result is that what a college or university calls a "learning community" often may not be a true learning community. Colleges and universities need to realize that creative new intentional approaches to learning communities are being developed that can greatly improve college students' learning. An anonymous reviewer of this report noted that "building communities as described in this writing, especially communities of learners, sets the ambience for life-giving and uplifting experiences necessary to advance an individual and a whole society. A serious study of this manuscript may even lead to a linking of networks of societies into a new, yet undiscovered [and] unmastered connection."

Colleges and universities need to become committed to selecting the model(s) best for their students and their situation, and learn how to implement it for optimum effectiveness. Cross-fertilization among two or more quite different learning communities provides a rich opportunity for enhancing learning through group activities. Only when a college or university is a true learning organization and contains true faculty learning communities can it expect to create faculty learning communities and student learning communities that will optimize students' learning and create other positive outcomes.

We have far to go in the development of optimal learning communities of all three basic types, but the powerful potential is clear if we commit ourselves to honest examination. This powerful potential is true even for the emerging concept of virtual learning communities. But good planning and assessment must play key roles in their development.

REFERENCES

The Educational Resources Information Center (ERIC) Clearing-house on Higher Education abstracts and indexes the current litera-ture on higher education for inclusion in ERIC's database and an-nouncement in ERIC's monthly bibliographic journal, *Resources in Education* (RIE). Most of these publications are available through the ERIC Document Reproduction Service (EDRS). For publications cited in this bibliography that are available from EDRS, ordering number and price code are included. Readers who wish to order a publication should write to the ERIC Document Reproduction Ser-vice, 7420 Fullerton Road, Suite 110, Springfield, Virginia 22153-2852. (Phone orders with VISA or MasterCard are taken at (800) 443-ERIC or (703) 440-1400.) When ordering, please specify the document (ED) number. Documents are available as noted in mi-crofiche (MF) and paper copy (PC). If you have the price code ready when you call, EDRS can quote an exact price. The last page of the latest issue of *Resources in Education* also has the current cost, listed by code.

Abrami, Philip C., B. Chambers, C. Poulsen, C. DeSimone, S. d'Apollonia, and J. Howden. 1995. *Classroom Connections: Understanding and Using Cooperative Learning.* Toronto: Harcourt Brace.

Acebo, Sandra C., and Karen Watkins. 1988. "Community College Faculty Development: Designing a Learning Organization." In *Enhancing Staff Development in Diverse Settings,* edited by Gor-don G. Darkenwald. New Directions for Continuing Education No. 38. San Francisco: Jossey-Bass.

Adams, Dennis M. 1996. *Cooperative Learning: Critical Thinking and Collaboration across the Curriculum.* 2d ed. Springfield, Ill.: Charles C. Thomas.

American College Personnel Association. 1994. *The Student Learn-ing Imperative: Implications for Student Affairs.* Washington, D.C.: Author.

American River College. 1994. "American River College Beacon Proj-ect. Student Catalyst Program: Peer-Assisted Learning." Final report. Sacramento, Calif.: Author. ED 393 516. 38 pp. MF–01; PC–02.

Anchors, Scott, K.B. Douglas, and M.K. Kasper. 1993. "Developing and Enhancing Learning Communities." In *Student Housing and Residential Life: A Handbook for Professionals Committed to Resi-dential Goals,* edited by Roger B. Winston, Jr., S. Anchors, and Associates. San Francisco: Jossey-Bass.

Andersen, Jim. 1995. *Courageous Teaching: Creating a Caring Community in the Classroom.* Thousand Oaks, Calif.: Corwin

Press. ED 380 449. 100 pp. MF–01; PC not available EDRS.

Anderson, Jim, and A. Lee. Spring 1995. "Literacy Teachers Learning a New Literacy: A Study of the Use of Electronic Mail in a Reading Education Class." *Reading Research and Instruction* 34(3): 222–38.

Angelo, Thomas A. May 1997. "The Campus as Learning Community: Seven Promising Shifts and Seven Powerful Levers." *AAHE Bulletin* 49(9): 3–6.

Angelo, Thomas A., and K.P. Cross. 1993. *Classroom Assessment Techniques: A Handbook for College Teachers.* 2d ed. San Francisco: Jossey-Bass.

Argyris, Christopher. 1990. *Overcoming Organizational Defenses.* Reading, Mass.: Addison-Wesley.

Aronson, Elliot, N. Blaney, C. Stephan, J. Sikes, and M. Snapp. 1978. *The Jigsaw Classroom.* Beverly Hills, Calif.: Sage.

Astin, Alexander W. 1984. "Student Involvement: A Developmental Theory for Higher Education." *Journal of College Student Personnel* 25(5): 297–308.

———. 1985. *Achieving Educational Excellence: A Critical Assessment of Priorities and Practices in Higher Education.* San Francisco: Jossey-Bass.

———. 1993a. "What Matters in College?" *Liberal Education* 79(4): 4–15.

———. 1993b. *What Matters in College? Four Critical Years Revisited.* San Francisco: Jossey-Bass.

Astin, Alexander W., W. Korn, and K. Green. 1987. "Retaining and Satisfying Students." *Educational Record* 68(1): 36–42.

Austin, Ann E., and R.G. Baldwin. 1991. *Faculty Collaboration: Enhancing the Quality of Scholarship and Teaching.* ASHE-ERIC Higher Education Report No. 7. Washington, D.C.: George Washington Univ., Graduate School of Education and Human Development. ED 346 805. 138 pp. MF–01; PC–06.

Baker, Paul, and K. Moss. April 1996. "Building Learning Communities through Guided Participation." *Primary Voices K–6* 4(2): 2–6.

Bank, Barbara J., R.L. Slavings, and B.J. Biddle. 1990. "Effects of Peer, Faculty, and Parental Influences on Students' Persistence." *Sociology of Education* 63(3): 208–25.

Barr, Karen, and B. Dailey. 1996. "From Teaching to Learning, from Managing to Leading: Facilitation Skills to Bridge the Gap." In *The Olympics of Leadership: Overcoming Obstacles, Balancing Skills, Taking Risks. Proceedings of the Annual International Conference of the National Community College Chair Academy.*

Phoenix: National Community College Chair Academy. ED 394
567. 9 pp. MF–01; PC–01.

Barr, Robert B., and J. Tagg. November/December 1995. "From
Teaching to Learning: A New Paradigm for Undergraduate
Education." *Change* 27(6): 13–25.

Bellah, R.N., R. Madsen, W.P. Sullivan, A. Swidler, and S.M. Tipton.
1985. *Habits of the Heart: Individualism and Commitment in
American Life.* New York: Harper & Row.

Bennis, Warren G. 1993. *An Invented Life.* Reading, Mass.: Addison-
Wesley.

Bertrand, Yves. 1994. "The Bermuda Triangle of Education." Paper
presented at an annual meeting of the American Educational
Research Association, April, New Orleans, Louisiana. ED 372
064. 16 pp. MF–01; PC–01.

Billson, Janet M. 1994. "Group Process in the College Classroom:
Building Relationships for Learning." In *Collaborative Learning:
A Sourcebook for Higher Education,* edited by Stephanie Kadel
and J.A. Keehner. Vol. 2. University Park, Penna.: National
Center on Postsecondary Teaching, Learning, and Assessment.

Blau, Peter M. 1994. *The Organization of Academic Work.* 2d ed.
New Brunswick, N.J.: Transaction.

Blumenstyk, Goldie. 10 July 1998. "Leading Community Colleges
Go National with New Distance-Learning Network." *Chronicle of
Higher Education* 44(44): A16–A17.

Bonwell, Charles C., and J.A. Eison. 1991. *Active Learning: Creating
Excitement in the Classroom.* ASHE-ERIC Higher Education Report No. 1. Washington, D.C.: George Washington Univ., Graduate School of Education and Human Development. ED 336 049.
121 pp. MF–01; PC–05.

Bonwell, Charles C., and T.E. Sutherland, eds. 1996. *Using Active
Learning in College Classes: A Range of Options for Faculty.* New
Directions for Teaching and Learning No. 67. San Francisco:
Jossey-Bass.

Bosworth, Kris, and S.J. Hamilton, eds. 1994. *Collaborative Learning:
Underlying Processes and Effective Techniques.* New Directions for
Teaching and Learning No. 59. San Francisco: Jossey-Bass.

Bouton, Clark, and R.Y. Garth, eds. 1983. *Learning in Groups.* New
Directions for Teaching and Learning No. 14. San Francisco:
Jossey-Bass.

Boyer Commission on Educating Undergraduates in the Research
University. 1998. *Reinventing Undergraduate Education: A Blue-
print for America's Research Universities.* Stony Brook: State University of New York at Stony Brook.

Boyer, Ernest L. 1987. *College: The Undergraduate Experience in America*. New York: Harper & Row.

———. 1990. *Scholarship Reconsidered: Priorities of the Professorate*. Princeton, N.J.: Princeton Univ. Press.

Brandt, Ronald C., ed. 1991. *Readings from Educational Leadership: Cooperative Learning and the Collaborative School*. Alexandria, Va.: Association for Supervision and Curriculum Development. ED 342 108. 219 pp. MF–01; PC not available EDRS.

Braxton, Joanne M., A. Sullivan, and R.M. Johnson. 1997. "Appraising Tinto's Theory of College Student Departure." In *Higher Education: Handbook of Theory and Research,* edited by John Smart. New York: Agathon Press.

Brody, Celest M. Winter 1995. "Collaborative or Cooperative Learning? Complementary Practices for Instructional Reform." *Journal of Staff, Program, and Organizational Development* 12(3): 133–43. ED 383 355. 266 pp. MF–01; PC not available EDRS.

Brosnan, Patricia A., and T.G. Ralley. 1995. "Impact of Calculus Reform in a Liberal Arts Calculus Course." Paper presented at an annual meeting of the North American Chapter of the International Group for the Psychology of Mathematics Education, October, Columbus, Ohio. ED 389 559. 7 pp. MF–01; PC–01.

Brown, Juanita B., B. Smith, and D. Isaacs. 1994. "Operating Principles for Building Community." In *The Fifth Discipline Fieldbook: Strategies and Tools for Building a Learning Organization,* edited by P. Senge, A. Kleiner, C. Roberts, R. Ross, and B. Smith. New York: Doubleday.

Brown, Judy Sorum. January/February 1997. "On Becoming a Learning Organization." *About Campus* 1(6): 5–10.

Brown, Lynn L, and S.E. Robinson Kurpius. November/December 1997. "Enhancing the Educational Impact of Residence Halls: The Relationship between Residential Learning Communities and First-Year College Experiences and Persistence." *Journal of College Student Development* 38(1): 11.

Brown, Rexford. 1997. "The Learning Organization: A Model for Educational Change." *NAMTA Journal* 22(1): 190–203.

Brubacher, John S., and S.W. Rudy. 1976. *Higher Education in Transition: A History of American Colleges and Universities, 1636–1976.* 3d ed. New York: Harper & Row.

Bruffee, Kenneth A. 1984. "Collaborative Learning and the 'Conversation of Mankind.'" *College English* 46: 635–52.

———. March/April 1987. "The Art of Collaborative Learning." *Change* 19(2): 42–47.

———. Spring 1988. "On Not Listening in Order to Hear: Col-

laborative Learning and the Rewards of Classroom Research."
Journal of Basic Writing 7(1): 3–12.

———. 1993. *Collaborative Learning in Higher Education: Interdependence and the Authority of Knowledge.* Baltimore: Johns
Hopkins Univ. Press.

———. January/February 1995. "Sharing Our Toys: Cooperative
Learning versus Collaborative Learning." *Change* 27(1): 12–19.

Burns, Marilyn. September 1981. "Groups of Four: Solving the
Management Problems." *Learning:* 46–51.

Caprio, Mario W. March/April 1993. "Cooperative Learning: The
Jewel among Motivational Teaching Techniques." *Journal of
College Science Teaching* 22(5): 279–81.

Carter, Judy H. 1995. "Dealing with Parasites in Group Projects."
Paper presented at an annual meeting of the Speech Communication Association, November, San Antonio, Texas. ED 392 100.
30 pp. MF–01; PC–02.

Chase, Dorothy D. 1991. "Using a Local Area Network and Other
Software with Adults." Paper presented at an annual meeting of
the International Reading Association, May, Las Vegas, Nevada.

Chickering, Arthur W. 1969. *Education and Identity.* San Francisco:
Jossey-Bass.

———. 1974. *Commuting versus Resident Students: Overcoming
Educational Inequities of Living Off Campus.* San Francisco:
Jossey-Bass.

Chickering, Arthur W., and Z.F. Gamson. 1987. "Seven Principles
for Good Practice in Undergraduate Education." *AAHE Bulletin*
39(7): 3–7.

Choi, Hyaeweol. 1995. *An International Scientific Community: Asian
Scholars in the United States.* Westport, Conn.: Greenwood Press.

Clark, Burton R., and M. Trow. 1966. "The Organizational Context."
In *College Peer Groups: Problems and Prospects of Research,*
edited by Theodore M. Newcomb and E.K. Wilson. Hawthorne,
N.Y.: Aldine.

Clement, John, and J. Abrahams. 1994. "Networking in 1993." *Educational Media and Technology Yearbook* 20: 106–19.

Cleveland, John, and P. Plastrik. 1995. "Learning Organizations and
TQM." In *Total Quality Management: Implications for Higher
Education,* edited by Allan M. Hoffman and D.J. Julius. Mary-
ville, Mo.: Prescott Publishing.

Cockrell, Karen S. July 1996. "Communication Gatekeeping: A Response to Mediating Conditions in American Indian and School
Personnel Interactions." *Journal of School Leadership* 6(4): 368–98.

Cohen, Carol. 1995. *Improving the Freshman College Classroom through Building a Purposeful Community of Altruistic and Motivated Learners.* Fort Lauderdale: Nova Southeastern Univ. ED 381 216. 90 pp. MF–01; PC–04.

Cohen, Elizabeth G. 1994a. *Designing Groupwork: Strategies for the Heterogeneous Classroom.* 2d ed. New York: Teachers College Press.

———. Spring 1994b. "Restructuring the Classroom: Conditions for Productive Small Groups." *Review of Educational Research* 64(1): 1–35.

Colbert, Joel A., P. Desberg, and K. Trimble, eds. 1996. *The Case for Education: Contemporary Approaches for Using Case Methods.* Boston: Allyn & Bacon.

Collison, Michele M. N-K. 10 November 1993. "Learning Communities for All." *Chronicle of Higher Education:* A18.

Cooke, Bryan P. 1994. "Rethinking Teaching and Testing: Quality in the Classroom." Paper presented at the Eastern Regional Competency-Based Education Consortium's Annual Total Quality Education Conference, March, Asheville, North Carolina. ED 367 406. 19 pp. MF–01; PC–01.

Cooper, James L., R. Mueck, M. McKinney, and P. Robinson. Winter 1991. "Cooperative/Collaborative Learning: Research and Practice at the Collegiate Level. Part 2." *Journal of Staff, Program, and Organizational Development* 9(4): 239–52.

Cooper, James, and P. Robinson. 1997a. *Cooperative Learning 101: An Introduction to Small-Group Instruction in Science, Mathematics, and Engineering and Technology (SMET).* Madison: Univ. of Wisconsin–Madison, National Institute for Science Education.

———. 1997b. "Small-Group Instruction: An Annotated Bibliography of Science, Mathematics, Engineering and Technology." Occasional Paper No. 6. Madison: Univ. of Wisconsin–Madison, National Institute for Science Education.

Cooper, Melanie M. 1995. "Cooperative Learning: An Approach for Large Enrollment Classes." *Journal of Chemical Education* 72(2): 162–65.

Cordeiro, Paula A, and B. Campbell. 1995. "Problem-Based Learning as Cognitive Apprenticeship in Educational Administration." Paper presented at an annual meeting of the American Educational Research Association, April, San Francisco, California. ED 386 800. 28 pp. MF–01; PC–02.

Cottle, Paul D., and G.E. Hart. 1996. "Cooperative Learning in the Tutorials of a Large Lecture Physics Class." *Research in Science Education* 26(2): 219–31.

Courtney, Daria Paul, M. Courtney, and C. Nicholson. 1994. "The

Effect of Cooperative Learning as an Instructional Practice at the College Level." *College Student Journal* 28: 471–77.

Cox, Barbara, ed. 1993. *Learning Communities in Teacher Education Programs: Four Success Stories.* Claremont, Calif.: Tomas River Center.

Coye, Dale. May/June 1997. "Ernest Boyer and the New American College: Connecting the 'Disconnects.'" *Change* 29(3): 20–29.

Cramer, Sharon Farago. 1994. "Assessing Effectiveness in the Collaborative Classroom." In *Collaborative Learning: Underlying Processes and Effective Techniques.* New Directions for Teaching and Learning No. 59. San Francisco: Jossey-Bass.

Crook, Charles. 1994. *Computers and the Collaborative Experience of Learning.* London: Routledge.

Crookston, Burns B. 1980. "A Design for an Intentional Democratic Community." In *Student Development and Education in College Residence Halls,* edited by D.A. DeCoester and P. Mable. Cincinnati: American College Personnel Association.

Cross, K. Patricia. July/August 1998. "Why Learning Communities? Why Now?" *About Campus* 3(3): 4–11.

Curry, Barbara K. 1992. *Instituting Enduring Innovations: Achieving Continuity of Change in Higher Education.* ASHE-ERIC Higher Education Report No. 7. Washington, D.C.: George Washington Univ., Graduate School of Education and Human Development. ED 358 809. 90 pp. MF–01; PC–04.

Cusack, Margaret S. November/December 1995. "Does Building a Classroom Community Facilitate Learning?" *Teaching PreK–8* 26(3): 64–65.

Dailey, Doreen, and T. Hassler. 1997. "A State-Level Catalyst for Transformation: Arizona Learning Systems." In *Mobilizing for Transformation,* edited by N. Norris and J. Morrison. New Directions for Institutional Research No. 94. San Francisco: Jossey-Bass.

Dale, Edgar. 1972. "Building a Learning Environment." Monograph Series No. 3. Bloomington, Ind.: Phi Delta Kappa Educational Foundation.

Daniel, Sir John S. July/August 1997. "Why Universities Need Technology Strategies." *Change* 29(4): 11–17.

Davidson, Neil, ed. 1990. *Cooperative Learning in Mathematics: A Handbook for Teachers.* Reading, Mass.: Addison-Wesley.

Davidson, Neil, and T. Worsham, eds. 1992. *Enhancing Thinking through Cooperative Learning.* New York: Teachers College Press.

Davies, Dick. August 1988. "Computer-Supported Cooperative Learning Systems: Interactive Group Technologies and Open

Learning." *Programmed Learning and Educational Technology* 25: 205–15.

Davis, Barbara Gross. 1993. *Tools for Teaching*. San Francisco: Jossey-Bass.

Devries, David L., K.J. Edwards, and R.E. Slavin. 1978. "Biracial Learning Teams and Race Relations in the Classroom: Four Field Experiments Using Teams-Games-Tournament." *Journal of Educational Technology* 70(3): 356–62.

Diefenbach, Lynnae P. 1996. "Learning Team Participation: The Effects on Pre-Business First-Year Students." Master's thesis, Iowa State Univ.

Dix, Jennifer. Fall 1996. "Reaching Out to Undergraduates: LS&A's Learning Communities." *USA Magazine:* 30–36.

Dudgeon, Carolyn. 1995. "Creating and Sustaining Learning Communities." *PHE Scholars Program Essays: Creating and Sustaining Learning Communities*. Fort Lauderdale: Nova Southeastern Univ., Center for the Advancement of Education. ED 386 118. 31 pp. MF–01; PC–02.

Dunn, Dana S., L. Rouse, and M.A. Seff. 1994. "New Faculty Socialization in the Academic Workplace." In *Higher Education: Handbook of Theory and Research*. Vol. 10, edited by John C. Smart. New York: Agathon Press.

Endo, Jean, and R.L. Harpel. 1982. "The Effect of Student-Faculty Interaction on Students' Educational Outcomes." *Research in Higher Education* 16(2): 115–38.

Fairweather, James S. 1996. *Faculty Work and Public Trust: Restoring the Value of Teaching and Public Service in American Academic Life*. Needham Heights, Mass.: Allyn & Bacon.

Felner, Robert. March 1997. "The Project on High Performance Learning Communities: Applying the Land-Grant Model to School Reform." *Phi Delta Kappan* 78(7): 520–27.

Finaly-Neumann, Edith, and Y. Neumann. 1995. "Quality Learning Teams: Improving Student Retention." In *Total Quality Management: Implications for Higher Education,* edited by Allan M. Hoffman and D.J. Julius. Maryville, Mo.: Prescott Publishing.

Fineman, Marcia P. 1996. "Learning Together." *Executive Educator* 18(5): 34–35.

Finley, Nancy J. 1990. "Meeting Expectations by Making New Connections: Curriculum Reform at Seattle Central." *Educational Record* 71(4): 50–53.

Fischer, Norman M. 1995. "The Long-Term Effects of Undergraduate Student Involvement Experiences on Selected Outcome Measures." Paper presented at an annual forum of the Association for Institutional Research, May, Baltimore, Maryland. ED 387 001. 23 pp. MF–01; PC–01.

Fowell, S.P., and P. Levy. September 1995. "Computer-Mediated Communication in the Information Curriculum: An Initiative in Computer-Supported Collaborative Learning." *Education for Information* 13(3): 193–210.

Franklin, Godfrey, et al. 1995. "Effects of Cooperative Tutoring on Academic Performance." *Journal of Educational Technology Systems* 23(1): 13–25.

Freed, Jann E., and M.R. Klugman. 1996. "Higher Education Institutions as Learning Organizations: The Quality Principles in Higher Education." Paper presented at an annual conference of the Association for the Study of Higher Education, November, Memphis, Tennessee. ED 402 845. 17 pp. MF–01; PC–01.

Freed, Jann E., M.R. Klugman, and J.D Fife. 1997. *A Culture for Academic Excellence: Implementing the Quality Principles in Higher Education.* ASHE-ERIC Higher Education Report No. 1. Washington, D.C.: George Washington Univ., Graduate School of Education and Human Development. ED 406 963. 200 pp. MF–01; PC–08.

Freemyer, Jan, et al. 1995. "Collaborative Learning at Glendale Community College." Glendale, Calif.: Glendale Community College. ED 388 364. 29 pp. MF–01; PC–02.

Freud, Robert. 1996. "Community Colleges and the Virtual Community." In *Issues of Education at Community Colleges: Essays by Fellows in the Mid-Career Fellowship Program at Princeton University,* edited by W. Allen Ashby. Princeton, N.J.: Princeton Univ., Center for Faculty Development. ED 397 868. 174 pp. MF–01; PC–07.

Friedlander, Jack, and P. MacDougall. 1991. "Achieving Student Success through Student Involvement." ED 329 310. 11 pp. MF–01; PC–01.

Gabelnick, Faith. January/February 1997. "Educating a Committed Citizenry." *Change* 29(1): 30–35.

Gabelnick, Faith, J. MacGregor, R.S. Matthews, and R.S. Smith. 1990. *Learning Communities: Creating Connections among Students, Faculty, and Disciplines.* New Directions for Teaching and Learning No. 41. San Francisco: Jossey-Bass.

Gaff, Jerry G., and J.L. Ratcliff, eds. 1997. *Handbook of the Undergraduate Curriculum: A Comprehensive Guide to Purposes, Structures, Practices, and Change.* San Francisco: Jossey-Bass.

Gamson, Zelda F. September/October 1994. "Collaborative Learning Comes of Age." *Change* 26(5): 44–49.

Gamson, Zelda F., and Associates. 1984. *Liberating Education.* San Francisco: Jossey-Bass.

Gardner, John W. Fall 1989. "Building Community." *Kettering Review:* 73–81.

———. 1990. *On Leadership.* New York: Free Press.

Gere, Anne Ruggles. 1987. *Writing Groups: History, Theory, and Implications. Studies in Writing and Rhetoric.* Carbondale: Southern Illinois Univ. Press.

Gibbs, Jeanne. 1994. *Tribes: A New Way of Learning Together.* Santa Rosa, Calif.: CenterSource Publications. ED 379 073. 425 pp. MF–01; PC not available EDRS.

———. 1995. *Tribes: A New Way of Learning and Being Together.* Sausalito, Calif.: CenterSource Systems.

Glover, Jeanette, and C.S. Hull-Toye. 1995. "Does JOBSWORK Work? Assessing the Effect of Student Involvement on Outcomes." Paper presented at an annual forum of the Association for Institutional Research, May, Boston, Massachusetts. ED 387 005. 25 pp. MF–01; PC–01.

Goodsell, Anne S., M. Maher, V. Tinto, B.L. Smith, and J. Mac-Gregor, eds. 1992. *Collaborative Learning: A Sourcebook for Higher Education.* University Park, Penna.: National Center on Postsecondary Teaching, Learning, and Assessment. ED 357 705. 175 pp. MF–01; PC–07.

Gore, Robert C. 1993. "Freshman Composition for the Learning Disabled." Paper presented at the Annual International Conference of the National Institute for Staff and Organizational Development on Teaching Excellence and Conference of Administrators, May, Austin, Texas. ED 361 026. 25 pp. MF–01; PC–01.

Gratton, Margaret. 1993. "Leadership in the Learning Organization." In *Changing Managerial Imperatives,* edited by Richard L. Alfred and Patricia Carter. New Directions for Community Colleges No. 84. San Francisco: Jossey-Bass.

Green, Kenneth. 1996. "Campus Computing, 1996. The Seventh National Survey of Desktop Computing and Information Technology in American Higher Education." Encino, Calif.: Campus Computing. ED 405 762. 38 pp. MF–01; PC not available EDRS.

Grineski, Steve. 1996. *Cooperative Learning in Physical Education.* Aukland, N.Z.: Human Kinetics.

Groff, Warren H. 1996. *Creating and Sustaining Learning Communities in the Digital Era.* Fort Lauderdale: Nova Southeastern Univ. ED 396 188. 368 pp. MF–01; PC–15.

Gutierrez, Kris D., and L.D. Stone. Spring 1997. "A Cultural-Historical View of Learning and Learning Disabilities: Participating in a Community of Learners." *Learning Disabilities Research and Practice* 12(2): 123–31.

Hagelgans, Nancy L., B.E. Reynolds, K. Schwingendorf, D. Vidakovic, E. Dubinsky, M. Shahin, and J.G. Wimbish, Jr., eds. 1995. *A Practical Guide to Cooperative Learning in Collegiate Mathematics.* MAA Notes No. 37. Washington, D.C.: Mathematical Association of America.

Hamilton, Sharon J. 1994. "Freedom Transformed: Toward a Developmental Model for the Construction of Collaborative Learning Environments." In *Collaborative Learning: Underlying Processes and Effective Techniques,* edited by Kris Bosworth and S.J. Hamilton. New Directions for Teaching and Learning No. 59. San Francisco: Jossey-Bass.

Hamilton, Stephanie L. 1997. "The Effects of a Residential Learning Community on First-Semester Biological Science Freshmen at a Traditional Land-Grant University." Master's thesis, Iowa State Univ.

Hannafin, Robert D., and W.C. Savenye. June 1993. "Technology in the Classroom: The Teacher's New Role and Resistance to It." *Educational Technology* 33(6): 26–31.

Hansen, W. Lee. April 1993. "Bringing Total Quality Improvement into the College Classroom." *Higher Education* 25(3): 259–79.

Harris, Zelema M., and P. Kayes. 1996. "New Statewide Regional Initiative on Creating Inclusive Educational Communities for Minority Students." Paper presented at an annual convention of the American Association of Community Colleges, April, Atlanta, Georgia. ED 397 891. 12 pp. MF–01; PC–01.

Hartley, James R. 1996. "Managing Models of Collaborative Learning." *Computers and Education* 26(1–3): 163–70.

Heath, Douglas. 1968. *Growing Up in College: Liberal Health Education and Maturity.* San Francisco: Jossey-Bass.

Hess, Marlene A. 1993. "Creating a Collaborative Context for Critical Thinking in Composition." Paper presented at an annual meeting of the Conference on College Composition and Communication, March, San Diego, California. ED 357 389. 10 pp. MF–01; PC–01.

Hill, Patrick. 1982. "Communities of Learners: Curriculum as the Infrastructure of Academic Communities." In *Opposition to the Core Curriculum: Alternative Models of Undergraduate Education,* edited by J.W. Hill and B.L. Kevles. Westport, Conn.: Greenwood Press.

Holland, John L. 1966. *The Psychology of Vocational Choice.* Waltham, Mass.: Blaisdell.

Hubbard, Dean L., and J.E. Gilmour. 1996. "The Malcolm Baldrige Criteria: A Structure for Converting Universities into Genuine Learning Organizations." In *High Performing Colleges: The Malcolm Baldrige National Quality Award as a Framework for Improving Higher Education.* Vol. 2, edited by Daniel Seymour et al. Maryville, Mo.: Prescott Publishing.

Hudson, Shirley A. 1995. "Enhancing Communication Skills in Team Projects." ED 387 617. 9 pp. MF–01; PC–01.

Hummel, Mary L. January/February 1997. "Eliminating the Achievement Gap: The 21st Century Program." *About Campus* 1(6): 28–29.

Hunter, Carol L. 1996. "Student as Teacher: Cooperative Learning Strategies in the Community College." In *Issues of Education at Community Colleges: Essays by Fellows in the Mid-Career Fellowship Program at Princeton University,* edited by W. Allen Ashby. Princeton, N.J.: Princeton Univ., Center for Faculty Development. ED 397 868. 174 pp. MF–01; PC–07.

Hunter, Gordon E. 1994. "Junior High School/College Collaborative Learning." *Innovation Abstracts* 16(4): 1. ED 375 918. 62 pp. MF–01; PC–03.

Hutchings, Patricia. 1993. *Using Cases to Improve College Teaching: A Guide to More Reflective Practice.* Washington, D.C.: American Association for Higher Education. ED 406 960. 86 pp. MF–01; PC not available EDRS.

International Association for the Study of Cooperation in Education. July 1991a. "Cooperative Learning and the Language Arts: Learning to Communicate—Communicating to Learn." *Cooperative Learning Magazine* 11(4).

———. April 1991b. "Cooperative Learning and Science." *Cooperative Learning Magazine* 11(3).

———. Fall 1992a. "Assessment in Cooperative Learning." *Cooperative Learning Magazine* 13(1).

———. February 1992b. "Staff Development: Building Communities of Learners." *Cooperative Learning Magazine* 12(2).

Iowa State University. 1995. "Strategic Plan for 1995–2000." Ames: Author.

Isaacs, William N. 1994. "Dialogue: The Power of Collective Thinking." In *Reflections on Creating Learning Organizations,* edited by K.T. Wardman. Cambridge, Mass.: Pegasus Communications.

Ishler, Richard E., and B. Vogel. November 1996. "The Celebration School: A Model Learning Community." *Principal* 76(2): 10–12.

Johnson, David W., et al. January 1981. "Effects of Cooperative, Competitive, and Individualistic Goal Structures on Achievement: A Meta-Analysis." *Psychological Bulletin* 89(1): 47–62.

Johnson, David W., and R.T. Johnson. 1975. *Learning Together and Alone: Cooperation, Competition, and Individualization.* Englewood Cliffs, N.J.: Prentice-Hall.

———. 1990. "Cooperative Learning and Achievement." In *Cooperative Learning: Theory and Practice,* edited by Shlomo Sharan. New York: Praeger.

———. 1993. "Implementing Cooperative Learning." *Education Digest* 58(8): 62–67.

———. 1994a. *Joining Together: Group Theory and Group Skills.* 5th ed. Englewood Cliffs, N.J.: Prentice-Hall.

———. 1994b. *Learning Together and Alone: Cooperative, Competitive, and Individualistic Learning.* 4th ed. Englewood Cliffs, N.J.: Prentice-Hall.

Johnson, David W., R.T. Johnson, and E. Holubec. 1994. *Circle of Learning: Cooperation in the Classroom.* Edina, Minn.: Interaction.

Johnson, David W., R.T. Johnson, and K.A. Smith. 1991a. *Active Learning: Cooperation in the College Classroom.* Edina, Minn.: Interaction.

———. 1991b. *Cooperative Learning: Increasing College Faculty Instructional Productivity.* ASHE-ERIC Higher Education Report No. 4. Washington, D.C.: George Washington Univ., Graduate School of Education and Human Development. ED 343 465. 168 pp. MF–01; PC–07.

———. July/August 1998. "Cooperative Learning Returns to College: What Evidence Is There That It Works?" *Change* 30(4): 26–35.

Johnstone, Sally M., and B. Krauth. March/April 1996. "Balancing Quality and Access: Some Principles of Good Practice for the Virtual University." *Change* 28(2): 38–41.

Kadel, Stephanie, and J.A. Keehner. 1994. *Collaborative Learning: A Sourcebook for Higher Education.* Vol. 2. University Park, Penna.: National Center on Postsecondary Teaching, Learning, and Assessment.

Kagan, Spencer. 1985. "Co-op Co-op: A Flexible Cooperative Learning Technique." In *Learning to Cooperate, Cooperating to Learn,* edited by Robert E. Slavin et al. New York: Plenum.

———. 1989. *Cooperative Learning.* San Juan Capistrano, Calif.: Resources for Teachers.

———. 1992. *Cooperative Learning.* 2d ed. San Juan Capistrano, Calif.: Resources for Teachers.

Kerka, Sandra. 1995. "The Learning Organization: Myths and Realities." Columbus, Ohio: ERIC Clearinghouse on Adult, Career, and Vocational Education. ED 388 802. 4 pp. MF–01; PC–01.

Kerns, Tim. May 1996. "Should We Use Cooperative Learning in College Chemistry?" *Journal of College Science Teaching* 25(6): 35–38.

Kessler, Carolyn, ed. 1992. *Cooperative Language Learning: A Teacher's Resource Book.* Englewood Cliffs, N.J.: Prentice-Hall.

Kirby, Donald J. 1991. "Dreaming Ambitious Dreams: The Values Program at LeMoyne College." *AAHE Bulletin* 43(6): 9–12.

Kluge, Lorene. 1990. *Cooperative Learning.* Arlington, Va.: Educational Research Service.

Knefelkamp, L. Lee. March/April 1992. "The Multicultural Curriculum and Communities of Peace." *Liberal Education* 78(2): 26–35.

Knight, George P., and E.M. Bohlmeyer. 1990. "Cooperative Learning and Achievement: Methods for Assessing Causal Mechanisms." In *Cooperative Learning: Theory and Practice,* edited by Shlomo Sharan. New York: Praeger.

Kofman, Fred, and P.M. Senge. 1993. "Communities of Commitment: The Heart of Learning Organizations." *Organizational Dynamics* 22(2): 5–22.

Kohlberg, Lawrence. 1971. "Stages of Moral Development." In *Moral Education,* edited by C.M. Beck, B.S. Crittenden, and E.V. Sullivan. Toronto: Univ. of Toronto Press.

Kolb, David. 1984. *Experiential Learning: Experiences as a Source of Learning and Development.* Englewood Cliffs, N.J.: Prentice-Hall.

———. 1985. *Self-Scoring Inventory and Interpretation Booklet.* Boston: McBer & Co.

Kouzes, James M. 1994. *Credibility.* San Francisco: Jossey-Bass.

Kouzes, James M., and B.Z. Posner. 1987. *The Leadership Challenges.* San Francisco: Jossey-Bass.

Krovetz, Martin L. 1993. "Collegial Learning Communities: The Road to School Restructuring." *School Community Journal* 3(2): 71–84.

Kuh, George D. 1994. "Creating Campus Climates That Foster Learning." In *Realizing the Educational Potential of Residence Halls,* edited by Charles C. Schroeder, P. Mable, and Associates. San Francisco: Jossey-Bass.

———. 1996a. "Guiding Principles for Creating Seamless Learning Environments for Undergraduates." *Journal of College Student Development* 37(2): 135–48.

———. 1996b. "Some Things We Should Forget." *About Campus* 1(4): 10–15.

Kuh, George, J.H. Schuh, E.J. Whitt, and Associates. 1991. *Involving Colleges: Successful Approaches to Fostering Student Learning and Development outside the Classroom*. San Francisco: Jossey-Bass.

Lamport, Mark A. Winter 1993. "Student-Faculty Informal Interaction and the Effect on College Student Outcomes: A Review of the Literature." *Adolescence* 28(112): 971–90.

Lander, Denis, et al. 1995. "A Practical Way of Structuring Teaching for Learning." *Higher Education Research and Development* 14(1): 47–59.

Laws, Priscilla W., et al. 1995. "Women's Responses to an Activity-Based Introductory Physics Program." In *Fostering Student Success in Quantitative Gateway Courses*, edited by J. Gainen and E.W. Willemsen. New Directions for Teaching and Learning No. 61. San Francisco: Jossey-Bass.

Lee, Terrence O. 1996. "Decentering the Freshman Composition Classroom: An Overview with Secondary Materials That Illustrate Student Success within the Classroom." Paper presented at an annual meeting of the Conference on College Composition and Communication, March, Milwaukee, Wisconsin. ED 397 427. 28 pp. MF–01; PC–02.

Lenski, Susan D. April 1996. "Honoring Student Self-Evaluation in the Classroom Community." *Primary Voices K–6* 4(2): 24–32.

Levine, Arthur. 1980. *When Dreams and Heroes Died: A Portrait of Today's College Student*. San Francisco: Jossey-Bass.

———, ed. 1993. *Higher Learning in America: 1980–2000*. Baltimore: Johns Hopkins Univ. Press.

Levine, Arthur, and J.S. Cureton. 1998. *When Hopes and Fear Collide: A Portrait of Today's College Student*. San Francisco: Jossey-Bass.

Levine, J.H., and D.P. Tompkins. June 1996. "Making Learning Communities Work: Seven Lessons from Temple University." *AAHE Bulletin* 48(10): 3–6.

Lieberman, Ann. November 1996. "Creating Intentional Learning Communities." *Educational Leadership* 54(3): 51–55.

Light, Richard. 1990. *The Harvard Assessment Seminars. First Report*. Cambridge, Mass.: Harvard Univ., Graduate School of Education.

Lin, Xiaodong. September/October 1995. "Instructional Design and Development of Learning Communities: An Invitation to a Dialogue." *Educational Technology* 35(5): 53–63.

Lippitt, Ronald. 1981. "Humanizing Planned Changes." In *Making Organizations Humane and Productive: A Handbook for Practitioners*, edited by J.H. Metzger and W. Nord. New York: Wiley.

Loehr, Peter. February 1994. "Creating Learning Organizations: The Demming Management Method Applied to Instruction." Mimeographed. ED 378 156. 30 pp. MF–01; PC–02.

Logan, Kent R. December 1994/January 1995. "How Inclusion Built a Community of Learners." *Educational Leadership* 52(7): 20–23.

Love, Anne Goodsell, and K.A. Tokuno. *In press.* "Learning Community Models." In *Learning Communities: New Structures, New Partnerships for Learning.* Columbia, S.C.: National Center for the Freshman Year Experience and Students in Transition.

Love, Patrick G., and A.G. Love. 1995. *Enhancing Student Learning: Intellectual, Social, and Emotional Integration.* ASHE-ERIC Higher Education Report No. 4. Washington, D.C.: George Washington Univ., Graduate School of Education and Human Development. ED 400 742. 166 pp. MF–01; PC–07.

Lucas, John A., and J. Mott. 1996. "Learning Communities' Impact on National Agenda Goals for Higher Education." Paper presented at an annual forum of the Association for Institutional Research, May, Albuquerque, New Mexico. ED 397 713. 24 pp. MF–01; PC–01.

Lucas, Robert. June 1998. "An Ecology of Distance Learning." *Syllabus* 11(10): 14–16+.

Lyman, Lawrence, H.C. Foyle, and T.S. Azwell. 1993. *Cooperative Learning in the Elementary Classroom.* Washington, D.C.: National Education Association. ED 367 461. 155 pp. MF–01; PC not available EDRS.

Lyons, Paul. 1995 "Classrooms as Learning Organizations: Challenging Assumptions and Processes." Mimeographed. ED 384 304. 13 pp. MF–01; PC–01.

McConnell, David. 1994. *Implementing Computer-Supported Cooperative Learning.* London: Kagan Page.

McCuen, Sharon, et al. January 1996. "Beacon PAL: Peer-Assisted Learning Project Update." New Beacon Outcomes Research Briefs No. 11. Sacramento, Calif.: American River College, Office of Research and Development. ED 393 517. 10 pp. MF–01; PC–01.

McEwan, A.E. 1993. "On Becoming a Sojourning Community." Paper presented at an annual meeting of the American Educational Research Association, April, Atlanta, Georgia. ED 359 914. 14 pp. MF–01; PC–01.

MacGregor, Jean. Fall 1991. "What Differences Do Learning Communities Make?" *Washington Center News* 6(1): 4–9.

MacGregor, Jean, B.L. Smith, R.S. Matthews, and F. Gabelnick. 1997. "Learning Community Models." Paper presented at an annual conference of the American Association for Higher Education, March, Washington, D.C.

MacKay, Jannie. 1996. *Establishing a Learning Community for Community College Students: STAR—Students and Teachers*

Achieving Results. Long Beach, Calif.: Long Beach City College. ED 393 514. 62 pp. MF–01; PC–03.

McLaughlin, Tim, and J. MacGregor. 1996. *Curricular Learning Communities Directory.* Olympia: Washington Center for Improving the Quality of Undergraduate Education.

McNeill, B.W., and L. Bellamy. 1995. *Engineering Core Workbook for Active Learning, Assessment, and Team Training.* ED 384 315. 231 pp. MF–01; PC–10.

Magid, Annette. 1988. "Cooperative Communication: A Study of Group Interaction." Paper presented at the Annual Symposium on Developmental/Remedial Education of the New York College Learning Skills Association, Catskills, New York. ED 297 797. 25 pp. MF–01; PC–01.

Male, Mary. 1994. "Cooperative Learning and Computers." In *Handbook of Cooperative Learning Methods,* edited by Shlomo Sharan. Westport, Conn.: Green Press.

Marchese, Theodore J. 1994. "Foreword." In *Realizing the Educational Potential of Residence Halls,* edited by Charles C. Schroeder, P. Mable, and Associates. San Francisco: Jossey-Bass.

Martin, Deanna C., and D.R. Arendale, eds. 1994. *Supplemental Instruction: Increasing Achievement and Retention.* New Directions for Teaching and Learning No. 60. San Francisco: Jossey-Bass.

Martin, Deanna C., and R.A. Blanc. 1994. "VSI: A Pathway to Mastery and Persistence." In *Supplemental Instruction: Increasing Achievement and Retention,* edited by Deanna C. Martin and D.R. Arendale. New Directions for Teaching and Learning No. 60. San Francisco: Jossey-Bass.

Masterson, John T. April 1998. "Learning Communities, the Wizard, and the Holy Grail." *AAHE Bulletin* 50(8): 8–9.

Matthews, Marian. 1992. "Gifted Students Talk about Cooperative Learning." *Educational Leadership* 50(2): 48–53.

Matthews, Roberta. October/November 1986. "Learning Communities in the Community College: How to Improve Student Involvement and Raise Faculty Morale." *Community, Junior, and Technical College Journal* 57(2): 44–47.

———. 1994. "Enriching Teaching and Learning through Learning Communities." In *Teaching and Learning in the Community College,* edited by Terry O'Banion. Washington, D.C.: American Association of Community Colleges. ED 368 416. 327 pp. MF–01; PC not available EDRS.

———. 1996a. "Collaborative Learning: Creating Knowledge with Students." In *Teaching on Solid Ground: Using Scholarship to Improve Practice,* edited by Robert J. Menges and M. Weimer.

University Park, Penna.: National Center on Postsecondary
Teaching, Learning, and Assessment.

————. 1996b. *Learning Communities: A Retention Strategy That
Serves Students and Faculty.* Washington, D.C.: American Association of State Colleges and Universities.

Matthews, Roberta S., J.L. Cooper, N. Davidson, and P. Hawkes.
July/August 1995. "Building Bridges between Cooperative and
Collaborative Learning." *Change* 27(4): 35–40.

Matthews, Roberta S., B.L. Smith, J. MacGregor, and F. Gabelnick.
1997. "Creating Learning Communities." In *Handbook of the
Undergraduate Curriculum: A Comprehensive Guide to Purposes,
Structures, Practices, and Change,* edited by Jerry G. Gaff and
J.L. Ratcliff. San Francisco: Jossey-Bass.

May, Susan. Fall 1994. "Beyond 'Super Secretary' Courses: Revisioning
Staff Development in Learning Organizations." *Canadian Journal
of University Continuing Education* 20(2): 45–54.

Meiklejohn, Alexander. 1932. *The Experimental College.* New York:
Harper & Row.

Merseth, Katherine K. 1991. *Case Studies in Teacher Education.*
New York: Harper Collins.

————. 1995. "Cases and Case Methods in Teacher Education." In
Handbook on Teacher Education. New York: Macmillan.

Meyers, Chet, and T.B. Jones. 1993. *Promoting Active Learning:
Strategies for the College Classroom.* San Francisco: Jossey-Bass.

Millis, Barbara J. Fall 1991. "Enhancing Adult Learning through
Cooperative Small Groups." *Continuing Higher Education Review* 55(3): 144–54.

————. 1995. "Introducing Faculty to Cooperative Learning." In
*Teaching Improvement Practices: Successful Strategies for Higher
Education,* edited by W.A. Wright. Bolton, Mass.: Anker.

————. 1997. *Cooperative Learning for Higher Education Faculty.*
Phoenix: Oryx Press.

Morris, Bill, ed. 1993. *Scintillating Suggestions for Involving Students: The Faculty Handbook for Student Involvement.* Sacramento, Calif.: American River College. ED 354 954. 81 pp.
MF–01; PC–04.

Moss, Kay. April 1996. "Reflections." *Primary Voices K–6* 4(2):
33–38.

Muhlhauser, Max, and T. Rudebusch. 1994. "Cooperation Support
in Computer-Aided Authoring and Learning." In *Educational
Multimedia and Hypermedia, 1994: Proceedings of ED-MEDIA
94—World Conference on Educational Multimedia and Hypermedia.* June, Vancouver, British Columbia. ED 388 276. 7 pp.

MF–01; PC–01.

Myers, Isabel B., and M. McCaulley. 1985. *A Guide to the Development and Use of the Myers-Briggs Type Indicator.* Gainesville, Fla.: Center for the Applications of Psychological Type.

Newcomb, Theodore M. 1966. *College Peer Groups: Problems and Prospects for Research.* Chicago: Aldine.

Nurrenbern, Susan C., ed. 1995. *Experiences in Cooperative Learning: A Collection for Chemistry Teachers.* Madison: Univ. of Wisconsin–Madison, Institute for Chemical Education.

O'Banion, Terry. 1997. *A Learning College for the 21st Century.* Washington, D.C.: Community College Press.

O'Malley, Clair, and E. Scanlon. 1989. *Computer-Supported Collaborative Learning: Problem Solving and Distance Education.* Report No. 75. Walton, Bletchley, Eng.: Bucks Institute of Technology, Center for Information Technology in Education.

O'Neil, John. April 1995. "On Schools as Learning Organizations: A Conversation with Peter Senge." *Educational Leadership* 52(7): 20–23.

Orbe, Mark P. 1995. "Building Community in the Diverse Classroom: Strategies for Communication Professors." Paper presented at an annual meeting of the Central States Communication Association, April, Indianapolis, Indiana. ED 387 838. 23 pp. MF–01; PC–01.

Orrange, Mary Beth. 1993. "Promoting Excellent Teaching: The Chair as Academic Leader." Paper presented at the Annual International Conference for Community College Chairs, Deans, and Other Instructional Leaders, February, Phoenix, Arizona.

Padilla, Raymond V., J. Trevino, K. Gonzalez, and J. Trevino. March/April 1997. "Developing Local Models of Minority Student Success in College." *Journal of College Student Development* 38(2): 125.

Pascarella, Ernest T. 1980. "Student-Faculty Informal Contact and College Outcomes." *Review of Educational Research* 50(4): 545–95.

Pascarella, Ernest T., and P.T. Terenzini. 1977. "Patterns of Student-Faculty Interaction beyond the Classroom and Voluntary Freshman Attrition." *Journal of Higher Education* 48(5): 540–52.

———. 1979. "Student-Faculty Informal Contact and College Persistence: A Further Investigation." *Journal of Educational Research* 72(4): 214–18.

———. 1983. "Predicting Voluntary Freshman Year Persistence/Withdrawal Behavior in a Residential University: A Path Analytic Validation of Tinto's Model." *Journal of Educational Psychology*

75(2): 215–26.

———. 1991. *How College Affects Students: Findings and Insights from Twenty Years of Research.* San Francisco: Jossey-Bass.

———. Winter 1998. "Studying College Students in the 21st Century: Meeting New Challenges." *Review of Higher Education* 21: 162.

Pascarella, Ernest T., P.T. Terenzini, and G.S. Blimling. 1994. "The Impact of Residential Life on Students." In *Realizing the Educational Potential of Residence Halls,* edited by Charles C. Schroeder, P. Mable, and Associates. San Francisco: Jossey-Bass.

Peck, M. Scott. 1987. *The Different Drum: Community Making and Peace.* New York: Simon & Schuster.

Perry, William G. 1970. *Forms of Intellectual and Ethical Development in the College Years: A Scheme.* New York: Holt, Rinehart & Winston.

Pfaff, Frank. Winter 1997. "The Era of Transformation: A Personal Tour of the 21st Century." *Magazine of St. Gregory's College* 2(4): 2–4.

Phipps, Shelley E. 1993. "Transforming Libraries into Learning Organizations: The Challenge of Leadership." *Journal of Library Administration* 18(3–4): 19–37.

Pike, Gary R. 1997. "The Effects of Residential Learning Communities on Students' Educational Experiences and Learning Outcomes during the First Year of College." Paper presented at an annual conference of the Association for the Study of Higher Education, November, Albuquerque, New Mexico. ED 415 828. 28 pp. MF–01; PC–02.

Pike, Gary R., C.C. Schroeder, and T.R. Berry. November/December 1997. "Enhancing the Educational Impact of Residence Halls: The Relationship between Residential Learning Communities and First-Year College Experience and Persistence." *Journal of College Student Development* 38(6): 609.

Pisani, Anoush M. 1994. "Involvement through Cooperative Learning: An Attempt to Increase Persistence in the Biological Sciences." Paper presented at an annual meeting of the Association for the Study of Higher Education, November, Tucson, Arizona. ED 375 723. 24 pp. MF–01; PC–01.

Pollio, H. 1984. "What Students Think About and Do in College Lecture Classes." Teaching-Learning Series No. 53. Knoxville: Univ. of Tennessee, Learning Research Center.

Powers, Susan M., and J. Mitchell. 1997. "Student Perceptions and Performance in a Virtual Classroom Environment." Paper presented at an annual meeting of the American Educational Research Association, March, Chicago, Illinois. ED 409 005. 25 pp.

MF–01; PC–01.

Prawat, Richard S. January/February 1996. "Learning Community, Commitment, and School Reform." *Journal of Curriculum Studies* 28(1): 91–110.

Price, Elsa C. 1994. "Comparing Community College Students' Learning Styles in General and Advanced Biology Classes." Paper presented at an annual meeting of the Association of Teacher Educators, February, Atlanta, Georgia. ED 394 929. 32 pp. MF–01; PC–02.

———. 1995. "On the Cutting Edge of Creativity: The Use of Art Projects in Community College Science Classes." Paper presented at an annual meeting of the Association of Teacher Educators, February, Detroit, Michigan. ED 394 928. 32 pp. MF–01; PC–02.

Purdom, Daniel M., and J.D. Kromrey. 1995. "Adapting Cooperative Learning Strategies to Fit College Students." *College Student Journal* 29: 57–64.

Putnam, Joanne W. 1993. *Cooperative Learning and Strategies for Inclusion: Celebrating Diversity in the Classroom.* Baltimore: Brookes Publishing.

Qin, Zhining, D.W. Johnson, and R.T. Johnson. Summer 1995. "Cooperative versus Competitive Efforts and Problem Solving." *Review of Educational Research* 65(2): 129–43.

Rapp, Rhonda H., and D.J. Gittinger. 1993. "Using Computers to Accommodate Learning-Disabled Students in Mathematics Classes." Paper presented at an annual conference of the League for Innovation in the Community College, November, Nashville, Tennessee. ED 364 272. 18 pp. MF–01; PC–01.

Ravitz, Jason. 1997. "An ISD Model for Building Online Communities: Furthering the Dialogue." Paper presented at a national convention of the Association for Educational Communications and Technology, February, Albuquerque, New Mexico. ED 409 863. 12 pp. MF–01; PC–01.

Regel, Pat. 1993. "Using a Total Quality Management Approach in the Teaching of English Composition." Paper presented at the Annual Computer Conference of the League for Innovation in the Community College, November, Nashville, Tennessee. ED 364 306. 52 pp. MF–01; PC–03.

Rendon, Laura I. Fall 1994. "Validating Culturally Diverse Students: Toward a New Model of Learning and Student Development." *Innovative Higher Education* 9(1): 33–51.

Robinson, Pamela, and J. Cooper. 1995. *An Annotated Bibliography of Cooperative Learning in Higher Education.* Part 3. *The 1990s.* Stillwater, Okla.: New Forums Press.

Rockwood, H.S. 1995a. "Cooperative and Collaborative Learning. Part 1." *National Teaching and Learning Forum* 4(6): 8–9.

———. 1995b. "Cooperative and Collaborative Learning. Part 2." *National Teaching and Learning Forum* 5(1): 8–10.

Romer, Karen T., and W.R. Whipple. Spring 1991. "Collaboration across the Power Line." *College Teaching* 39(2): 66–70.

Rose, Arthur L. 1994. "A Semester in the Library with an English 087 Class: A Partnership between Teacher, Students, and Librarians." Cranford, N.J.: Union County College. ED 387 194. 15 pp. MF–01; PC–01.

Roychoudhury, Anita, and W.F. Roth. Spring 1992. "Student Involvement in Learning: Collaboration in Science for Preservice Elementary Teachers." *Journal of Science Teacher Education* 3(2): 47–52.

Rutledge, Carolyn. July/August 1996. "The Learning Community: A Pro-Family System of Education and Community Support." *Adult Learning* 7(6): 9–10.

Ryan, Mark B. September/October 1992. "Residential Colleges: A Legacy of Living and Learning Together." *Change* 24(5): 26–35.

Ryan, S. 1994. "The Emergence of Learning Communities." In *Reflections on Creating Learning Organizations,* edited by K.T. Wardman. Cambridge, Mass.: Pegasus Communications.

St. Gregory's College. *n.d. The Renaissance Plan: A Comprehensive Plan for the Renewal of St. Gregory's College.* Shawnee, Okla.: Author.

Sanford, Nevitt. 1962. *The American College.* New York: Wiley.

Schneider, Carol Geary. 1997. "The Arts and Sciences Major." In *Handbook of the Undergraduate Curriculum: A Comprehensive Guide to Purposes, Structures, Practices, and Change,* edited by J.G. Gaff and J.L. Ratcliff. San Francisco: Jossey-Bass.

Schoem, David, ed. 1993. *Multicultural Teaching in the University.* Westport, Conn.: Greenwood Publishing Group.

Schroeder, Charles C. 1993. "Conclusion. Creating Residence Life Programs with Student Development Goals." In *Student Housing and Residential Life: A Handbook for Professionals Committed to Residential Goals,* edited by Roger B. Winston, Jr., S. Anchors, and Associates. San Francisco: Jossey-Bass.

———. 1994. "Developing Learning Communities." In *Realizing the Educational Potential of Residence Halls,* edited by Charles C. Schroeder, P. Mable, and Associates. San Francisco: Jossey-Bass.

Schroeder, Charles C., and J.C. Hurst. 1996. "Designing Learning Communities That Integrate Curricular and Cocurricular Experiences." *Journal of College Student Development* 37(2): 174–81.

Schroeder, Charles C., P. Mable, and Associates, eds. 1994. *Realizing the Educational Potential of Residence Halls.* San Francisco: Jossey-Bass.

Schumm, Jeanne Shay. 1993. "What Gifted Students Think about Cooperative Learning." *Journal of Reading* 36(7): 549–50.

Seabreeze, John R. 1997. "Student Affairs World Wide Web Sites." New Directions for Student Services No. 78. San Francisco: Jossey-Bass.

Secules, Teresa. March 1997. "Creating Schools for Thought." *Educational Leadership* 54(6): 56–60.

Sego, Arlene. 1991. *Cooperative Learning: A Classroom Guide.* Cleveland: Info Tech.

Senge, Peter M. 1990. *The Fifth Discipline: The Art and Practice of the Learning Organization.* New York: Doubleday.

———. 1994a. "Creating Quality Communities." *Executive Excellence* 11(6): 11–13.

———. 1994b. "The Leader's New Work: Building Learning Organizations." In *CQI 101: A First Reader for Higher Education.* AAHE's Continuous Quality Improvement Project. Washington, D.C.: American Association for Higher Education.

Senge, Peter M., A. Kleiner, C. Roberts, R.B. Ross, and B.J. Smith, eds. 1994. *The Fifth Discipline Fieldbook: Strategies and Tools for Building a Learning Organization.* New York: Doubleday.

Sharan, Shlomo. 1980. "Cooperative Learning in Small Groups: Recent Methods and Effects on Achievement, Attitudes, and Ethnic Relations." *Review of Educational Research* 50(2): 241–71.

———, ed. 1994. *Handbook of Cooperative Learning Methods.* Westport, Conn.: Green Press.

Sharan, Schlomo, Y. Bejano, P. Kussell, and R. Peley. 1984. "Cooperative and Competitive Behavior." In *Cooperative Learning in the Classroom: Research in Desegregated Schools,* edited by Schlomo Sharan et al. Hillsdale, N.J.: Erlbaum.

Sharan, Shlomo, and R. Hertz-Lazarowitz. 1980. "A Group Investigation Method of Cooperative Learning in the Classroom." In *Cooperation in Education,* edited by Schlomo Sharan et al. Provo, Utah: Brigham Young Univ. Press.

Sharan, Shlomo, and Y. Sharan. 1976. *Small Group Teaching.* Engelwood Cliffs, N.J.: Educational Technology Publications.

———. 1992. *Expanding Cooperative Learning through Group Investigation.* New York: Teachers College Press.

Sharan, Yael, and S. Sharan. December 1989/January 1990. "Group Investigation Expands Cooperative Learning." *Educational Leadership* 47: 17–22.

Shaw, Walter B. 1975. "The Residence Hall as a Community in Higher Education." New York: Educational Facility Labs. ED 100 056. 11 pp. MF–01; PC–01.

Shields, Carolyn M. January 1996. "Creating a Learning Community in a Multicultural Setting: Issues of Leadership." *Journal of School Leadership* 5(1): 47–74.

Shulman, Judith H. 1992. *Case Methods in Teacher Education.* New York: Teachers College Press.

Shulman, Judith H., R.A. Lotan, and J.A. Whitcomb. 1995. *Group-work in Diverse Classrooms: A Casebook for Educators.* San Francisco: Far West Lab for Educational Research and Development. ED 394 944. 204 pp. MF–01; PC–09.

Silverman, Robert, W.M. Welty, and S. Lyon. 1992. *Case Studies for Teacher Problem Solving.* New York: McGraw-Hill.

Simpson, Grant W. 1995. "Cooperative Learning with Adults: Don't Assume Anything." *Adult Learning* 6(4): 10–12.

Slavin, Robert E. 1978. "Structured Teams and Achievement Divisions." *Journal of Research and Development in Education* 12: 39–49.

———. Summer 1980. "Cooperative Learning." *Review of Educational Research* 50(2): 315–42.

———. 1983a. *Cooperative Learning.* New York: Longman.

———. 1983b. "When Does Cooperative Learning Increase Student Achievement?" *Psychological Bulletin* 94: 429–45.

———. 1985. "Team-Assisted Individualization: Combining Cooperative Learning and Individualized Instruction in Mathematics." In *Learning to Cooperate, Cooperating to Learn,* edited by Robert E. Slavin et al. New York: Plenum.

———. 1991a. "Cooperative Learning and the Cooperative School." In *Cooperative Learning and the Collaborative School,* edited by Ronald S. Brandt. Alexandria, Va.: Association for Supervision and Curriculum Development. ED 342 108. 219 pp. MF–01; PC not available EDRS.

———. 1991b. *Student Team Learning.* 3d ed. Washington, D.C.: National Education Association.

———. 1995. *Cooperative Learning: Theory, Research, and Practice.* 2d ed. New York: Allyn & Bacon.

Slavin, Robert E., M.B. Leavey, and N.A. Madden. March 1984. "Cooperative Integrated Reading and Individualized Instruction: Effects on Student Mathematics Achievement, Attitudes, and Behaviors." *Elementary School Journal* 84: 409–22.

Smith, Barbara L. 1991. "Taking Structure Seriously: The Learning Community Model." *Liberal Education* 77(2): 42–48.

———. 1993. "Creating Learning Communities." *Liberal Education* 79(4): 32–39.

Smith, Barbara L., and J.T. MacGregor. 1992. "What Is Collaborative Learning?" In *Collaborative Learning: A Sourcebook for Higher Education,* edited by Anne S. Goodsell, M. Maher, V. Tinto, B.L. Smith, and J. MacGregor. University Park, Penna.: National Center for Postsecondary Teaching, Learning, and Assessment. ED 357 705. 175 pp. MF–01; PC–07.

Smith, Terry B. 1994. "Integrating Living and Learning in Residential Colleges." In *Realizing the Educational Potential of Residence Halls,* edited by Charles C. Schroeder, P. Mable, and Associates. San Francisco: Jossey-Bass.

Sollisch, James. May 1988. "Collaborative Learning: At the Intersection of Reading, Writing, and Response." *Teaching English at the Two-Year College* 15(2): 99–104.

Speck, Marsha. Spring/Summer 1996. "The Change Process in a School Learning Community." *School Community Journal* 6(1): 69–79.

Springer, Leonard, M.E. Stanne, and S. Donovan. 1997. *Effects of Cooperative Learning on Academic Achievement among Undergraduates in Science, Mathematics, Engineering, and Technology: A Meta-Analysis.* Madison: Univ. of Wisconsin–Madison, National Institute for Science Education.

Springer, Leonard, P.T. Terenzini, E.T. Pascarella, and A. Nora. 1995. "Influences on College Students' Orientations toward Learning for Self-Understanding." *Journal of College Student Development* 36(1): 5–18.

Stahl, Robert J., ed. 1994. *Cooperative Learning in the Social Sciences: A Handbook for Teachers.* New York: Addison-Wesley.

Stark, Joan S., and L.R. Lattuca. 1997. *Shaping the College Curriculum: Academic Plans in Action.* Needham Heights, Mass.: Allyn & Bacon.

Steinbrink, John E., and R.M. Stahl. 1994. "Jigsaw III = Jigsaw II + Cooperative Test Review: Applications to the Social Studies Classroom." In *Cooperative Learning in the Social Sciences: A Handbook for Teachers,* edited by Robert J. Stahl. New York: Addison-Wesley.

Study Group on the Conditions of Excellence in American Higher Education. 1984. *Involvement in Learning: Realizing the Potential of American Higher Education.* Washington, D.C.: U.S. Dept. of Education, National Institute of Education. ED 246 833. 127 pp. MF–01; PC–06.

Sullivan, Timothy M. 1994. "Creating and Sustaining Learning

Communities." In *PHE Scholars Program Essays: Creating and Sustaining Learning Communities.* Fort Lauderdale: Nova Southeastern Univ., Center for the Advancement of Education. ED 386 118. 31 pp. MF–01; PC–02.

Super, Donald E. 1957. *The Psychology of Careers.* New York: Harper-Collins.

Sykes, Gary, and T. Bird. 1992. "Teacher Education and the Case Idea." In *Review of Research in Education,* edited by Grace E. Grant. Washington, D.C.: American Educational Research Association.

Tebo-Messina, Margaret. Spring 1993. "Collaborative Learning: How Well Does It Work?" *Writing on the Edge* 4(2): 63–79.

Terenzini, Patrick T., and E.T. Pascarella. 1994. "Living with Myths: Undergraduate Education in America." *Change* 26(1): 28–32.

Terenzini, Patrick T., E.T. Pascarella, and G.S. Blimling. 1996. "Students' Out-of-Class Experiences and Their Influence on Learning and Cognitive Development: A Literature Review." *Journal of College Student Development* 37(2): 149–62.

Terenzini, Patrick T., L. Springer, P.M. Yaeger, E.T. Pascarella, and A. Nora. 1996. "First-Generation College Students: Characteristics, Experiences, and Cognitive Development." *Research in Higher Education* 37(1): 1–22.

Terenzini, Patrick T., and T.M. Wright. 1987. "Influences on Students' Academic Growth during Four Years of College." *Research in Higher Education* 26(2): 161–79.

Tiberius, Richard G. 1990. *Small Group Teaching: A Trouble-Shooting Guide.* Monograph Series No. 22. Toronto: Ontario Institute of Studies in Education.

Tinto, Vincent. 1988. "Stages of Student Departure: Reflections on the Longitudinal Character of Student Leaving." *Review of Higher Education* 59(4): 438–55.

———. 1990. "Principles of Effective Retention." *Journal of the Freshman Year Experience* 2(1): 35–48.

———. 1993. *Leaving College: Rethinking the Causes and Cures of Student Attrition.* Chicago: Univ. of Chicago Press.

———. 1997a. "Colleges as Communities: Exploring the Educational Character of Student Persistence." *Journal of Higher Education* 68(6): 599–623.

———. January/February 1997b. "Universities as Learning Organizations." *About Campus* 1(6): 2–4.

———. Winter 1998. "Colleges as Communities: Taking Research on Student Persistence Seriously." *Review of Higher Education* 21(2): 167–77.

Tinto, Vincent, and A.G. Love. 1993. "Freshman Interest Groups and the First-Year Experience: Constructing Student Communities in a Large University." Washington, D. C.: Office of Educational Research and Improvement. ED 358 778. 19 pp. MF–01; PC–01.

———. 1994. "Freshman Interest Groups and the First-Year Experience: Constructing Student Communities in a Large University." *Journal of the Freshman Year Experience* 6(1): 7–28.

———. 1995. *A Longitudinal Study of Learning Communities at LaGuardia Community College.* Washington, D.C.: Office of Educational Research and Improvement. ED 380 178. 213 pp. MF–01; PC–09.

Tinto, Vincent, A.G. Love, and P. Russo. 1993. "Building Community." *Liberal Education* 79(4): 16–21.

———. 1994. *Building Learning Communities for New College Students: A Summary of Research Findings of the Collaborative Learning Project.* University Park, Penna.: National Center for Postsecondary Teaching, Learning, and Assessment.

Tinto, Vincent, and P. Russo. 1994. "Coordinated Studies Programs: Their Effect on Student Involvement at a Community College." *Community College Review* 22: 16–26.

Tinto, Vincent, P. Russo, and S. Kadel. 1994. "Constructing Educational Communities: Increasing Retention in Challenging Circumstances." *Community College Journal* 64(4): 26–29.

Tokuno, Kenneth A. 1993. "Long-Term and Recent Student Outcomes of the Freshman Interest Groups." *Journal of the Freshman Year Experience* 2: 7–28.

Treisman, P. Uri. 1985. "A Study of the Mathematics Performance of Black Students at the University of California–Berkeley." Doctoral dissertation, Univ. of California–Berkeley.

Treuer, Paul, and L. Belote. 1997. "Current and Emerging Applications of Technology to Promote Student Involvement and Learning." In *Using Technology to Promote Student Learning: Opportunities for Today and Tomorrow,* edited by Catherine McHugh Engstrom and K.W. Kruger. New Directions for Student Services No. 78. San Francisco: Jossey-Bass.

Trimble, Kimberly. April 1996. "Building a Learning Community." *Equity and Excellence in Education* 29(1): 37–40.

Tussman, Joseph. 1969. *Experiment at Berkeley.* London: Oxford Univ. Press.

Twigg, Carol A., and D.G. Oblinger. 1997. *The Virtual University: A Report from a Joint Educom/IBM Roundtable.* Washington, D.C.: Educom.

Tyler, Deidre A. 1993. "At-Risk Nontraditional Community College Students." Paper presented at the Annual International Conference of the National Institute for Staff and Organizational Development in Teaching Excellence and Conference of Administrators, May, Austin, Texas. ED 361 055. 15 pp. MF–01; PC–01.

University of Missouri–Columbia. 1997. *Missouri FIGs and Other Learning Communities: Living and Learning.* Columbia: Author.

Upcraft, M. Lee 1993. "Translating Theory into Practice." In *The Handbook of Student Affairs Administrators,* edited by Margaret Barr. San Francisco: Jossey-Bass.

Upcraft, M. Lee, J.M. Gardner, and Associates. 1989. *The Freshman Year Experience: Helping Students Survive and Succeed in College.* San Francisco: Jossey-Bass.

Van Der Karr, Carol A. 1994. "Lessons Learned from Study Groups: Collaboration, Cooperation, and Involvement among Community College Students." Paper presented at an annual meeting of the Association for the Study of Higher Education, November, Tucson, Arizona. ED 375 719. 31 pp. MF–01; PC–02.

Waldorf College. Summer 1997. "Waldorf B.A. Graduates Finding Acceptance in the Work Force." *Waldorf College Magazine* 93(2): 15.

Warren, Roland L., and L. Lyon, eds. 1988. *New Perspectives on the American Community.* 5th ed. Chicago: Dorsey.

Warren, Russel G. March/April 1997. "Engaging Students in Active Learning." *About Campus* 2(1): 16–20.

Washington Center for Improving the Quality of Undergraduate Education. 1996. "The Washington Center Learning Communities Dissemination Project." Olympia: Author.

Weihl, Richard A. August–November 1995. *Thresholds in Education* 22(3–4): 21–28.

Weissglass, Julian. April 1996. "Transforming Schools into Caring Learning Communities." *Journal for a Just and Caring Education* 2(2): 175–89.

Wheatley, Margaret J. 1994. *Leadership and the New Science: Learning about Organization from an Orderly Universe.* San Francisco: Barrett-Kochler.

Wheeler, David. 1995. "Use of Learning Groups for Active Learning." In *Teaching of Psychology: Ideas and Innovations,* edited by David Griese and J.R. Levine. Farmingdale, N.Y.: State University of New York at Farmingdale. ED 389 364. 174 pp. MF–01; PC–07.

Whipple, Edward G., ed. 1998. *New Challenges for Greek Letter Organizations: Transforming Fraternities and Sororities into*

Learning Communities. New Directions for Student Services No. 81. San Francisco: Jossey-Bass.

Whipple, Edward G., and E.G. Sullivan. 1998. "Greek Letter Organizations: Communities of Learners." In *New Challenges for Greek Letter Organizations: Transforming Fraternities and Sororities into Learning Communities,* edited by Edward G. Whipple. New Directions for Student Services No. 81. San Francisco: Jossey-Bass.

Whitt, Elizabeth J., and E.M. Nuss. 1994a. "Connecting Residence Halls to the Curriculum." In *Realizing the Educational Potential of Residence Halls,* edited by Charles C. Schroeder, P. Mable, and Associates. San Francisco: Jossey-Bass.

———. 1994b. "Encouraging Adult Learner Involvement." *NASPA Journal* 31(4): 309–18.

Wilson, Charles E. 1996. *The Effects of Cooperative Learning and Teaching Strategies on Student Achievement.* Fort Lauderdale: Nova Southeastern Univ. ED 395 622. 113 pp. MF–01; PC–05.

Wingspread Group on Higher Education. 1993. *An American Imperative: Higher Expectations for Higher Education.* Racine, Wis.: Johnson Foundation. ED 364 144. 177 pp. MF–01; PC–08.

Winston, Roger B., Jr., S. Anchors, and Associates, eds. 1993. *Student Housing and Residential Life: A Handbook for Professionals Committed to Residential Goals.* San Francisco: Jossey-Bass.

Winston, Roger B., W.C. Bonney, T.H. Miller, and J.C. Dagley. 1988. *Promoting Student Development through Intentionally Structured Groups.* San Francisco: Jossey-Bass.

Wolfson, Gloria K. 1995. "Creating and Sustaining Learning Communities: The Electronic Learning Community." In *PHE Scholars Program Essays: Creating and Sustaining Learning Communities.* Fort Lauderdale: Nova Southeastern Univ., Center for the Advancement of Education. ED 386 118. 31 pp. MF–01; PC–02.

Wolf-Wendel, Lisa E. March/April 1998. "Models of Excellence: The Baccalaureate Origins of Successful European American Women, African-American Women, and Latinas." *Journal of Higher Education* 69: 178.

Woods, Donald R. 1996. *Bringing Problem-Based Learning to Higher Education: Theory and Practice.* New Directions for Teaching and Learning No. 68. San Francisco: Jossey-Bass.

Wulff, Donald H., J.D. Nyquist, and R.D. Abott. 1987. "Students' Perception of Large Classes." In *Teaching Large Classes Well,* edited by Maryellen G. Weimer. San Francisco: Jossey-Bass.

INDEX

courses, best mix of for student learning communities, 82–83

CQI. *See also* continuous quality improvement.

/TQM conceptual framework, 95

cross-curricular learning communities, 17–19

as learning community, 8

directory of, 18

important function of, 17–18

types of, 18

typology for, 19

Clark and Trow (1966) typology of students, 46

CSEQ. *See* College Student Experiences Questionnaire.

curricular learning communities, 16, 17–28

curricular area learning communities, 26–28

curricular cohort learning communities, 23–26

D

Davis (1993) on cooperative learning, 31

Delta College, 45

Deming, Dr. W. Edwards, 92

developing community to maximize learning, 8

developing student learning communities

how to get faculty involved in, 76–77

developmental model for constructing collaborative learning environments, 67

Dewey, John

focus on the value of learning within a community, 6

proponent of learning through community, 1

dialogue effectiveness of group members key to system thinking, 95

disciplined community, 7

discontinuity, times of, 7

Drexel University, 27–28, 80

E

Earlham College

exemplary in connecting residence halls with curriculum, 42

Eckerd College, 9

effective dialogue among group members key to system thinking, 95

electronic learning communities

four factors related to performance and perceptions, 101

e-mail, value of, 103

empirical and symbolic modes of inquiry

learning communities structured around, 42

entering student learning communities, 17

ERIC Clearinghouse on Higher Education, study cosponsored by, 95

Evergreen State College, 9, 17, 21–22

experimental undergraduate colleges, 9

F

facilitator, instructor as, 29

faculty

        benefits of learning communities, 56–57

        development, 68–70

        how to get involved in developing student learning

            communities, 76

        involvement, appropriate level of, 83

        learning communities, 11, 96–98

        resources for collaborative and cooperative learning, 66–68

Fairweather's categories of faculty behavior, 97–98

federated learning communities (FLCs), 18, 21–22

FIGs. *See* freshman interest groups.

Fine Arts Residential College, 43

First-Time College Students Community, 43

firsthand experience, real understanding comes only through, 29

fostering a community of learners, 33

fraternities and sororities,

        as the opposite of learning communities, 2

French and Spanish Language Houses, 43

freshman-experience learning communities, 42

freshman interest groups, 18, 19

        residential version of, 42–43

Fund for the Improvement of Postsecondary Education (FIPSE), 10, 88

furniture of the mind, 7

G

Gabelnick et al., five models of cross-curricular learning

    communities, 19–23

George Washington University, study cosponsored by, 95

global village, 5

great books approach to leadership development, 30

group investigation, 36–37

        six stages of implementation, 37

groups of four, 34

Gruenewald, Doug

        influential in improving learning communities at ISU, 74

H

Harvard University

        residential colleges at, 9

        student groups in residence halls effect on outcomes, 52

high-risk students, how learning communities can help, 81

higher education, increased focus on community in, 5–7

Hill, Patrick

        creator of federated learning communities, 21

honors

residence, 43
students learning community, 45
humanness model, 102

I

implementation of learning communities, ISU problems with, 71–72
initiative importance, 62
institution as learning organization
importance for student learning communities of, 93–94
institutional mission statement
importance of incorporating specific objectives into, 78
instructional system design (ISD), 100
integration between any two dimensions as typology for cross-curricular learning communities, 19
"intentional democratic values"
learning communities structured around, 42
Interdisciplinary Writing Program, 20
intergroup competition
less productive for cooperative goal structures, 60
International House, 43
Internet II, possible implications of emergence of, 107
Involvement in Learning, 5
involvement model, 49
involvement theory, 46
Iowa Central Community College, 107
Iowa Communication Network, 107
Iowa State University (ISU), 68
case study, 70–75
grant to support learning communities at, 74–75

J

Jigsaw I, II, and III, 35–36
Johnson, Johnson, and Smith
handbook on college professors' use of cooperative learning, 33
just community, 6

K

K–12 model for developing classroom community relevance, 29
Kansas City Community College, 59
Kellogg Foundation grant, 30
Kirkwood Community College, 107
Kolb's Learning Styles Inventory, 46

L

LaGuardia Community College, 17, 45, 55

mental models, 90

Michigan Learning Communities at the University of Michigan, 43

Michigan State University

    exemplary in connecting residence halls with curriculum, 42

model emphasizing problem-based learning of curricular area learning community, 27

models of student learning communities, results, 15

multicultural learning communities, 42

Myers-Briggs Type Inventory, 46

N

National Center for Postsecondary Teaching, Learning, and Assessment, 53, 55

    two books on collaborative learning from, 68

national clearinghouse on learning communities, 10

network of 20 adopting institutions, project to create, 88

"new American college," three priorities for, 89

New College at the University of Alabama, 9

new R's, 29

nonparticipants in student groups, tactics to get them involved, 65

Northeast Missouri State University

    living/learning colleges developed at, 42

O

Oklahoma State Regents for Higher Education

    electronic campus being developed by, 106

open community, 6

operating principles for building community, 95–96

operating procedures, seven positive shifts in, 91

organizational changes required of institutions, 94

organizational management. *See* management of human resources program.

Oxford residential colleges, 9

P

paired or clustered classes model, 18

Parker 19th century proponent of learning through community, 1

personal transformation, nothing happens without, 92

Phi Theta Kappa Leadership Development Studies course at Bacone College as total-classroom learning community, 30

physical interaction, 11

planning needs for development of learning communities, 79

positive interdependence, necessary conditions for, 79

primary form of interaction

    three basic categories of, 11–12

    of learning communities, 10

primary membership

  dimension of learning communities, 10–11

  types of learning communities not mutually exclusive, 11

program seminar, 22

purposeful community, 6

Q

Quintilian as proponent of learning through community, 1

R

reflection rubric, 69

residence halls

  as opportunity to improve student achievement, 41

  impact of residential learning communities upon, 84–85

Residential College/Honors Program, 44

residential learning communities, 17, 40–44

retention rate higher among learning community students, 52–53

S

Scholars Program at the University of Maryland–College Park, 43–44

scholarship of engagement, 89

Schroeder's models for creating authentic communities, 84

Seattle Central Community College, 55

Senge, Peter

  application of disciplines, 94–96

  five learning disciplines, 90

service-learning communities, 42

  as ultimate learning community, 85

seven positive shifts in operating procedures, 91–92

seven proven levers, 91

Shapiro, Howard

  jointly led faculty learning group on improving learning, 73

shared culture or common purpose, what to do if campus lacks, 76

shared knowing or knowledge

  as common to most learning communities, 10

shared vision, 90

skills needed by instructors to facilitate group collaboration, 69

Smart Catalog of Western Governors University, 105

software packages needed for collaborative learning within learning community, 102

Southern Regional Education Board, 105

Southern Regional Electronic Campus, 105

special focused colleges graduate disproportionate numbers of women who earn a doctoral degree, 47

special learning community project Biology Education Success Teams, 72

ASHE-ERIC HIGHER EDUCATION REPORTS

Since 1983, the Association for the Study of Higher Education (ASHE) and the Educational Resources Information Center (ERIC) Clearinghouse on Higher Education, a sponsored project of the Graduate School of Education and Human Development at The George Washington University, have cosponsored the ASHE-ERIC Higher Education Report series. This volume is the twenty-sixth overall and the ninth to be published by the Graduate School of Education and Human Development at The George Washington University.

Each monograph is the definitive analysis of a tough higher education problem, based on thorough research of pertinent literature and institutional experiences. Topics are identified by a national survey. Noted practitioners and scholars are then commissioned to write the reports, with experts providing critical reviews of each manuscript before publication.

Eight monographs (10 before 1985) in the ASHE-ERIC Higher Education Report series are published each year and are available on individual and subscription bases. To order, use the order form on the last page of this book.

Qualified persons interested in writing a monograph for the ASHE-ERIC Higher Education Report series are invited to submit a proposal to the National Advisory Board. As the preeminent literature review and issue analysis series in higher education, the Higher Education Reports are guaranteed wide dissemination and national exposure for accepted candidates. Execution of a monograph requires at least a minimal familiarity with the ERIC database, including *Resources in Education* and the current *Index to Journals in Education.* The objective of these reports is to bridge conventional wisdom with practical research. Prospective authors are strongly encouraged to call at (800) 773-3742 ext. 14.

For further information, write to
    ASHE-ERIC Higher Education Report Series
    The George Washington University
    One Dupont Circle, Suite 630
    Washington, DC 20036-1183
Or phone (202) 296-2597
Toll free: (800) 773-ERIC

Write or call for a complete catalog.

Visit our Web site at **www.eriche.org**

ADVISORY BOARD

James Earl Davis
University of Delaware at Newark

Kenneth A. Feldman
State University of New York–Stony Brook

Kassie Freeman
Peabody College, Vanderbilt University

Susan Frost
Emory University

Kenneth P. Gonzalez
Arizona State University

Esther E. Gotlieb
West Virginia University

Philo Hutcheson
Georgia State University

Lori White
Stanford University

Ivan B. Liss
Radford University

Anne Goodsell Love
University of Akron

Clara M. Lovett
Northern Arizona University

Meredith Ludwig
American Association of State Colleges and Universities

William McKeachie
University of Michigan

Jean MacGregor
Evergreen State College

Laurence R. Marcus
Rowan College

Robert Menges
Northwestern University

Diane E. Morrison
Centre for Curriculum, Transfer, and Technology

John A. Muffo
Virginia Polytechnic Institute and State University

Patricia H. Murrell
University of Memphis

L. Jackson Newell
University of Utah

Steven G. Olswang
University of Washington

R. Eugene Rice
American Association for Higher Education

Sherry Sayles-Folks
Eastern Michigan University

Maria Scatena
St. Mary of the Woods College

John Schub
Wichita State University

Jack H. Schuster
Claremont Graduate School–Center for Educational Studies

Carole Schwinn
Jackson Community College

Patricia Somers
University of Arkansas at Little Rock

Leonard Springer
University of Wisconsin–Madison

Marilla D. Svinicki
University of Texas–Austin

David Sweet
OERI, U.S. Department of Education

Jon E. Travis
Texas A&M University

Dan W. Wheeler
University of Nebraska–Lincoln

Donald H. Wulff
University of Washington

Manta Yorke
Liverpool John Moores University

William Zeller
University of Michigan at Ann Arbor

REVIEW PANEL

Richard Alfred
University of Michigan

Robert J. Barak
Iowa State Board of Regents

Alan Bayer
Virginia Polytechnic Institute and State University

John P. Bean
Indiana University–Bloomington

John M. Braxton
Peabody College, Vanderbilt University

Ellen M. Brier
Tennessee State University

Dennis Brown
University of Kansas

Patricia Carter
University of Michigan

John A. Centra
Syracuse University

Paul B. Chewning
Council for the Advancement and Support of Education

Arthur W. Chickering
Vermont College

Darrel A. Clowes
Virginia Polytechnic Institute and State University

Deborah M. DiCroce
Piedmont Virginia Community College

Dorothy E. Finnegan
The College of William & Mary

Kenneth C. Green
Claremont Graduate University

James C. Hearn
University of Georgia

Edward R. Hines
Illinois State University

Deborah Hunter
University of Vermont

Linda K. Johnsrud
University of Hawaii at Manoa

Bruce Anthony Jones
University of Missouri–Columbia

Elizabeth A. Jones
West Virginia University

Marsha V. Krotseng
State College and University Systems of West Virginia

George D. Kuh
Indiana University–Bloomington

J. Roderick Lauver
Planned Systems International, Inc.–Maryland

Daniel T. Layzell
MGT of America, Inc., Madison, Wisconsin

Patrick G. Love
Kent State University

Meredith Jane Ludwig
American Association of State Colleges and Universities

Mantha V. Mehallis
Florida Atlantic University

Toby Milton
Essex Community College

John A. Muffo
Virginia Polytechnic Institute and State University

L. Jackson Newell
Deep Springs College

Mark Oromaner
Hudson Community College

James C. Palmer
Illinois State University

Robert A. Rhoads
Michigan State University

G. Jeremiah Ryan
Quincy College

Mary Ann Danowitz Sagaria
The Ohio State University

Kathryn Nemeth Tuttle
University of Kansas

Volume 26 ASHE-ERIC Higher Education Reports

1. Faculty Workload Studies: Perspectives, Needs, and Future Directions
   Katrina A. Meyer

2. Assessing Faculty Publication Productivity: Issues of Equity
   Elizabeth G. Creamer

3. Proclaiming and Sustaining Excellence: Assessment as a Faculty Role
   Karen Maitland Schilling and Karl L. Schilling

4. Creating Learning Centered Classrooms: What Does Learning Theory Have to Say?
   Frances K. Stage, Patricia A. Muller, Jillian Kinzie, and Ada Simmons

5. The Academic Administrator and the Law: What Every Dean and Department Chair Needs to Know
   J. Douglas Toma and Richard L. Palm

Volume 25 ASHE-ERIC Higher Education Reports

1. A Culture for Academic Excellence: Implementing the Quality Principles in Higher Education
   Jann E. Freed, Marie R. Klugman, and Jonathan D. Fife

2. From Discipline to Development: Rethinking Student Conduct in Higher Education
   Michael Dannells

3. Academic Controversy: Enriching College Instruction through Intellectual Conflict
   David W. Johnson, Roger T. Johnson, and Karl A. Smith

4. Higher Education Leadership: Analyzing the Gender Gap
   Luba Chliwniak

5. The Virtual Campus: Technology and Reform in Higher Education
   Gerald C. Van Dusen

6. Early Intervention Programs: Opening the Door to Higher Education
   Robert H. Fenske, Christine A. Geranios, Jonathan E. Keller, and David E. Moore

7. The Vitality of Senior Faculty Members: Snow on the Roof— Fire in the Furnace
   Carole J. Bland and William H. Bergquist

8. A National Review of Scholastic Achievement in General Education: How Are We Doing and Why Should We Care?
   Steven J. Osterlind

Volume 24 ASHE-ERIC Higher Education Reports

1. Tenure, Promotion, and Reappointment: Legal and Administrative Implications
   Benjamin Baez and John A. Centra

2. Taking Teaching Seriously: Meeting the Challenge of Instructional Improvement
   Michael B. Paulsen and Kenneth A. Feldman

3. Empowering the Faculty: Mentoring Redirected and Renewed
   Gaye Luna and Deborah L. Cullen

4. Enhancing Student Learning: Intellectual, Social, and Emotional Integration
   Anne Goodsell Love and Patrick G. Love

5. Benchmarking in Higher Education: Adapting Best Practices to Improve Quality
   Jeffrey W. Alstete

6. Models for Improving College Teaching: A Faculty Resource
   Jon E. Travis

7. Experiential Learning in Higher Education: Linking Classroom and Community
   Jeffrey A. Cantor

8. Successful Faculty Development and Evaluation: The Complete Teaching Portfolio
   John P. Murray

Volume 23 ASHE-ERIC Higher Education Reports

1. The Advisory Committee Advantage: Creating an Effective Strategy for Programmatic Improvement
   Lee Teitel

2. Collaborative Peer Review: The Role of Faculty in Improving College Teaching
   Larry Keig and Michael D. Waggoner

3. Prices, Productivity, and Investment: Assessing Financial Strategies in Higher Education
   Edward P. St. John

4. The Development Officer in Higher Education: Toward an Understanding of the Role
   Michael J. Worth and James W. Asp II

5. Measuring Up: The Promises and Pitfalls of Performance Indicators in Higher Education
   Gerald Gaither, Brian P. Nedwek, and John E. Neal

6. A New Alliance: Continuous Quality and Classroom Effectiveness
   Mimi Wolverton

7. Redesigning Higher Education: Producing Dramatic Gains in Student Learning
   Lion F. Gardiner

8. Student Learning outside the Classroom: Transcending Artificial Boundaries
   George D. Kuh, Katie Branch Douglas, Jon P. Lund, and Jackie Ramin-Gyurnek

Volume 22 ASHE-ERIC Higher Education Reports

1. The Department Chair: New Roles, Responsibilities, and Challenges
   Alan T. Seagren, John W. Creswell, and Daniel W. Wheeler

2. Sexual Harassment in Higher Education: From Conflict to Community
   Robert O. Riggs, Patricia H. Murrell, and JoAnne C. Cutting

3. Chicanos in Higher Education: Issues and Dilemmas for the 21st Century
   Adalberto Aguirre, Jr., and Ruben O. Martinez

4. Academic Freedom in American Higher Education: Rights, Responsibilities, and Limitations
   Robert K. Poch

5. Making Sense of the Dollars: The Costs and Uses of Faculty Compensation
   Kathryn M. Moore and Marilyn J. Amey

6. Enhancing Promotion, Tenure, and Beyond: Faculty Socialization as a Cultural Process
   William G. Tierney and Robert A. Rhoads

7. New Perspectives for Student Affairs Professionals: Evolving Realities, Responsibilities, and Roles
   Peter H. Garland and Thomas W. Grace

8. Turning Teaching into Learning: The Role of Student Responsibility in the Collegiate Experience
   Todd M. Davis and Patricia Hillman Murrell

Quantity   **Amount**

_____ Please begin my subscription to the current year's
ASHE-ERIC Higher Education Reports at $144.00, 25%
off the cover price, starting with Report 1.   _____

_____ Please send a complete set of Volume 27 (Year 2000)
ASHE-ERIC Higher Education Reports at $144.00, over
25% off the cover price.   _____

Individual reports are available for $24.00 and include the cost of ship-
ping and handling.

 SECURE ON-LINE ORDERING
is now available on our web site.
www.eriche.org/reports

SHIPPING POLICY:

• Books are sent UPS Ground or equivalent. For faster delivery, call for
charges. Alaska, Hawaii, U.S. Territories, and Foreign Countries, please
call for shipping information. Order will be shipped within 24 hours
after receipt of request. Orders of 10 or more books, call for shipping
information. All prices shown are subject to change.

• Returns: No cash refunds—credit will be applied to future orders.

PLEASE SEND ME THE FOLLOWING REPORTS:

Quantity	Volume/No.	Title	Amount

Please check one of the following:

☐ Check enclosed, payable to GW-ERIC.

☐ Purchase order attached.

☐ Charge my credit card indicated below:

   ☐ Visa   ☐ MasterCard

Subtotal:	
Less Discount:	
Total Due:	

Expiration Date_____

Name_____

Title _____ E-mail _____

Institution _____

Address_____

City _____ State _____ Zip_____

Phone _____ Fax _____Telex_____

Signature _____ Date_____

SEND ALL ORDERS TO:
ASHE-ERIC Higher Education Reports Series
One Dupont Cir., Ste. 630, Washington, DC 20036-1183
Phone: (202) 296-2597 ext. 13 Toll-free: (800) 773-ERIC ext. 13
FAX: (202) 452-1844
EMAIL: order@eric-he.edu
Secure on-line ordering at URL: www.eriche.org/reports

**Secure on-line ordering
is available:
visit our web site at
www.eriche.org/reports**